Contents

Introduction

Active Maths 1 is a comprehensive new three-year textbook covering the complete Project Maths syllabus (Strands 1–5) for the Junior Certificate Ordinary Level course. On completing *Active Maths 1*, Higher Level students can continue the Junior Certificate Higher Level course with *Active Maths 2*.

Throughout the *Active Maths 1* textbook, there are links to this accompanying Activity Book.

The Project Maths approach is reflected throughout in the emphasis on directed investigative learning. This promotes real understanding of the topic and allows students to cope with context-based questions. Teachers will find that very few additional resources or photocopying are needed.

There are many reasons a teacher would choose to introduce these activities, either in the lesson or for homework:

- These real-life examples bring maths to life and show you how it relates to the world in which you live.
- Activities help you to understand each topic better before you tackle the questions on that topic.
- You will be better prepared for the kinds of questions you will see in the exam if you are used to doing these kinds of activities.
- Doing these activities can also help you to revise a topic.

We hope you enjoy these activities as much as we have enjoyed using them in our classes.

Good luck!

Michael Keating, Derek Mulvany and James O'Loughlin

Activity 1.1

1. Match the items in Column A with those in Column B.

A	B
A set	∈
~~List method~~	The number of elements in a set
'Is an element of'	A collection of well-defined objects
~~Rule method~~	∉
Cardinal number, #	The objects that make up a set
'Is not an element of'	All the elements of the set are listed inside curly brackets.
Elements	Using words to describe the elements of a set

2. $N = \{1, 2, 3, 4, ...\}$ $\qquad$ $Q = \{\text{Numbers of the form } \frac{a}{b}, a, b \in Z, b \neq 0\}$

$Z = \{..., -3, -2, -1, 0, 1, 2, 3, ...\}$ $\qquad$ $P = \{\text{The set of prime numbers}\}$

Say whether the following statements are true or false:

Statement	True/False
(i) Q is the set of all fractions.	True
(ii) N is the set of positive whole numbers.	True
(iii) Z is the set of integers.	True
(iv) Any number that has two and only two divisors is an element of P.	True
(v) $-1 \in N$	False
(vi) $-1 \in Q$	True
(vii) All the elements of P are also elements of N.	True
(viii) $13 \notin P$	False
(ix) $\#N = 4$	False

$$\frac{-1}{1}$$

Activity 1.2

1. S = {1, 2, 3, 4}

(i) Write out the four subsets of S that have only one element.

{   }, {   }, {   }, {   }

(ii) Write out the six subsets of S that have only two elements.

{   }, {   }, {   }, {   }, {   }, {   }

(iii) Write out the four subsets of S that have three elements.

{   }, {   }, {   }, {   }

(iv) Write out the improper subset of S.   {   }

(v) How many subsets does S have?

2. A = {v, w, x, y, z}

The set A has 10 subsets with three elements. Eight of the subsets are listed below. Find the remaining subsets containing three elements.

{v, w, x}, {v, w, y}, {v, w, z}, {v, x, y}, {v, y, z}, {w, x, y}, {w, x, z}, {w, y, z}, {   }, {   }

3. How many subsets do each of the following sets have? Write your answer in the form 2^n, where $n \in N$.

(i) {a, b, c, d, e}

(iv) {a, b, c, d, e, f, g, h}

(ii) {a, b, c, d, e, f}

(v) {a, b, c, d, e, f, g, h, i}

(iii) {a, b, c, d, e, f, g}

Activity 1.3

1. In the Venn diagram below, shade the set A ∪ B.

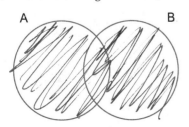

2. In the Venn diagram below, shade the set A ∩ B.

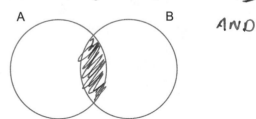

AND

3. Is A ∪ B = B ∪ A? Explain your reasoning.

4. Is A ∩ B = B ∩ A? Explain your reasoning.

If A ∪ B = B ∪ A, we say that ∪ is a commutative operation.

If A ∩ B = B ∩ A, we say that ∩ is a commutative operation.

Activity 1.4

1. U = {1, 2, 3, 4, 5, 6}

E = {2, 4, 6}

P = {2, 3, 5}

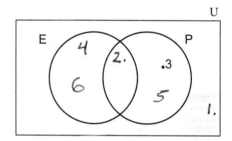

(i) Complete the Venn diagram.

(ii) E ∪ P = {2, 4, 6, 3, 5}   (iv) #(E ∪ P) = 5

(iii) E ∩ P = {2}   (v) #(E ∩ P) = 1

2. U = {1, 2, 3, 4, 5, 6, 7, 8, 9}

O = {1, 3, 5, 7, 9}

S = {1, 4, 9}

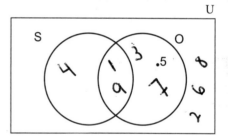

(i) Complete the Venn diagram.

Using your Venn diagram, find the following:

(ii) O ∪ S = {4, 1, 9, 3, 7, 5}   (v) S \ O = {4}

(iii) O ∩ S = {1, 9}   (vi) Is #(O \ S) = #(S \ O)? Explain.

(iv) O \ S = {3, 5, 7}

No

3. U = {a, b, c, d, e, f, g, h, i}

A = {a, c, e, g}

B = {b, d, f, h}

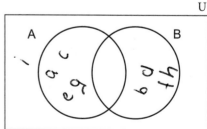

(i) Complete the Venn diagram.

Using your Venn diagram, find the following:

(ii) A ∪ B = {a, c, e, g, b, d, f, h}   (v) B \ A = {b, d, f, h}

(iii) A ∩ B = ∅   {}   (vi) A' = {i, b, d, f, h}

(iv) A \ B = {a, c, e, g}   (vii) (A ∪ B)' = {i}

Natural Numbers

Magic Squares

Write the numbers 1 to 9 so that each row, column and diagonal add up to **15**.

(i)

4	9	2
3	5	7
8	1	6

(iv)

4	3	8
9	5	1
2	7	6

(ii)

6	1	8
7	5	3
2	9	4

(v)

2	7	6
9	5	1
4	3	8

(iii)

2	7	6
9	5	1
4	3	8

(vi)

2	7	6
9	5	1
4	3	8

The **Sieve of Eratosthenes** is a method for finding all prime numbers up to a certain number. The 'sieve' was invented by an ancient Greek mathematician called Eratosthenes.

Example: The Sieve of Eratosthenes

Find all prime numbers less than 30 using the Sieve of Eratosthenes.

Step 1

Construct a rectangular grid containing the numbers 1 to 30.

1	2	3	4	5	6	7	8	9	10
11	12	13	14	15	16	17	18	19	20
21	22	23	24	25	26	27	28	29	30

Step 2

- Cross off 1, as it is not a prime number.
- Circle 2, the first prime number, and cross off all multiples of 2.
- Now, if 2^2 is less than 30, which it is, we continue to Step 3.

~~1~~	②	3	~~4~~	5	~~6~~	7	~~8~~	9	~~10~~
11	~~12~~	13	~~14~~	15	~~16~~	17	~~18~~	19	~~20~~
21	~~22~~	23	~~24~~	25	~~26~~	27	~~28~~	29	~~30~~

Step 3

- Circle the next number that is not crossed out, which is 3.
- Cross off all multiples of 3.
- Is 3^2 less than 30? Yes! Move to Step 4.

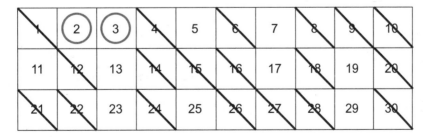

Step 4

- Circle the next number that is not crossed out, which is 5.
- Cross off all multiples of 5.
- Is 5^2 less than 30? Yes! Move to Step 5.

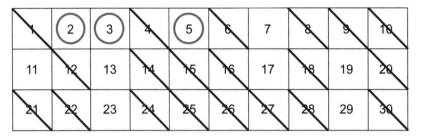

Step 5

- Circle the next number that is not crossed out, which is 7.
- Cross off all multiples of 7.

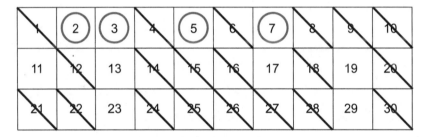

- Is 7^2 less than 30? No! We are finished. Circle all the remaining uncrossed numbers. All circled numbers are the prime numbers less than 30.

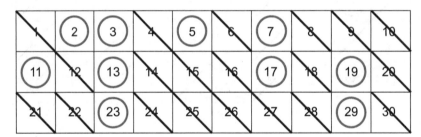

Using the grid below, and the method of Eratosthenes, circle all the prime numbers between 1 and 100.

(i) How many prime numbers are there between 1 and 100?

(ii) Write down all the prime numbers between 1 and 100.

Composite Numbers

All natural numbers greater than 1 that are not prime are called composite numbers. For example, 8 and 55 are composite numbers.

(iii) How many composite numbers are in the 1 to 100 grid?

(iv) Write down all the composite numbers between the two primes 23 and 29.

Twin Primes

A pair of prime numbers that have just one composite number between them are called twin primes. For example, 29 and 31 are twin primes, as 30 is the only composite number between 29 and 31.

(v) Are 11 and 13 twin primes? Explain your answer.

(vi) Are 31 and 37 twin primes? Explain your answer.

(vii) How many twin primes are there between 1 and 100?

(viii) Write down all the twin primes between 1 and 100.

Activity 2.3

1. Complete the factor table below. The factors of 12 and 18 have been done for you.

	1	2	3	4	5	6	7	8	9	10	11	12	13	14	15	16	17	18	19
19																			19
18																		18	
17																	17		
16																16			
15															15				
14														14					
13													13						
12												12							
11											11								
10										10									
9									9									9	
8								8											
7							7												
6						6						6						6	
5					5														
4				4								4							
3			3									3						3	
2		2										2						2	
1	1	1	1	1	1	1	1	1	1	1	1	1	1	1	1	1	1	1	1

2. Using the completed factor table, answer the questions that follow.

(i) How many factors does 10 have?

(ii) Which numbers between 1 and 20 have 3 as a factor?

(iii) How many numbers between 1 and 20 have just two factors?

(iv) Which two numbers between 1 and 20 have six factors?

(v) What is the highest common factor of 12 and 16?

NATURAL NUMBERS

Euclid, another famous ancient Greek mathematician, proved that every natural number greater than 1 is either a prime number or a product of prime numbers. For example:

$$50 = 2 \times 5 \times 5 = 2 \times 5^2$$

Example

Write 1,200 as a product of primes.

Solution

Factor trees are useful for writing a number as a product of primes. We begin by dividing 1,200 into a factor pair, then divide each factor into a factor pair. Continue in this way until all the factors are prime numbers. The product of all the prime numbers on the factor tree is the prime factorisation of 1,200.

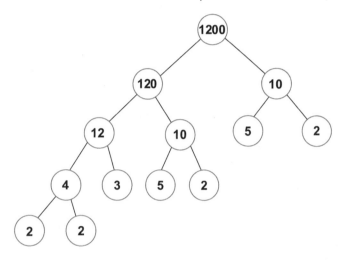

Therefore $1,200 = 2 \times 2 \times 2 \times 2 \times 3 \times 5 \times 5 = 2^4 \times 3 \times 5^2$.

1. Use factor trees to find the prime factorisation of the following numbers:

38	76	68	48

NATURAL NUMBERS

2. Use factor trees to find the prime factorisation of the following numbers:

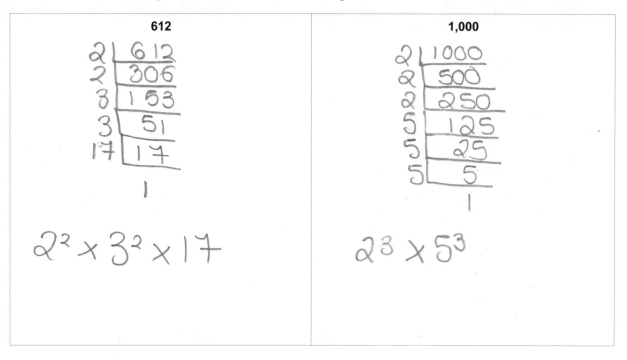

612	1,000

$$2^2 \times 3^2 \times 17 \qquad 2^3 \times 5^3$$

3. Find the LCM of each of the following pairs of numbers by writing the numbers as a product of primes.

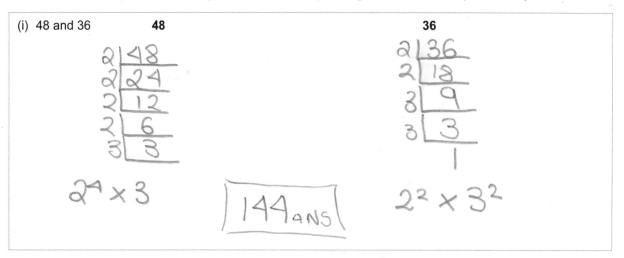

(i) 48 and 36

48   36

$2^4 \times 3$ $\boxed{144_{ANS}}$ $2^2 \times 3^2$

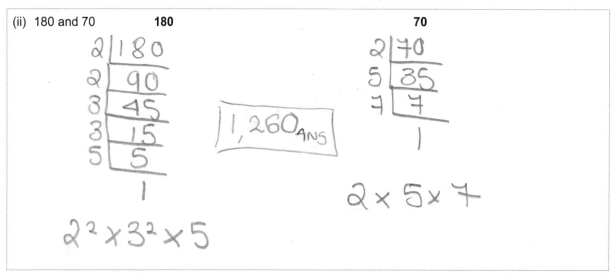

(ii) 180 and 70

180   70

$\boxed{1,260_{ANS}}$

$2^2 \times 3^2 \times 5 \qquad 2 \times 5 \times 7$

The Fundamental Principle of Counting

chapter 3

Activity 3.1

These are two **dice**.

In the table below, list all the possible outcomes of rolling two dice. There should be 36 outcomes.

1, 1					
2, 1					
			3, 4		
				5, 5	
	6, 2				

Activity 3.2

In the table below, list all the letters of the English alphabet.

(i) How many letters are in the alphabet? _____

(ii) List the letters that are vowels. _____

(iii) How many vowels are there? _____

(iv) What is the name given to the other types of letters?

_____

(v) How many of this type are there? _____

Activity 3.3

These are various types of coins.

When flipping or tossing a coin, there are two outcomes. What names do we give to these two outcomes?

_____ and _____

Activity 3.4

1. This is a pack, or deck, of cards (excluding Jokers).

(i) How many cards are in a pack of cards? _____

(ii) The pack is divided up into four different types, called **suits**. The suits are called _____,

_____, _____ and _____.

(iii) How many cards are in each suit? _____

2. The Jack is called a **picture card**.

(i) Can you identify the other picture cards?

_____ and _____

(ii) How many picture cards in total are there in a deck of cards?

_____

(Remember that there are four suits.)

Activity 3.5

This an example of a spinner.

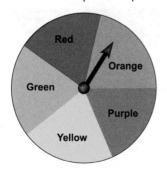

(i) How many sectors are there? _____

(ii) What colour sector has the arrow on the spinner stopped

at? _____

The number system we use has 10 **digits**: 0, 1, 2, 3, 4, 5, 6, 7, 8 and 9.

> The word 'digit' comes from the Latin *digita*, which means 'fingers'.

The number 12 is a two-digit number.

How many digits are in each of the following numbers?

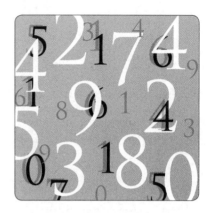

Number	Digits
147	
23,692	
9,841	
1,000,000	

 Activity 3.7

A coin is flipped twice. Fill in all the possible outcomes in the table below.

First throw	Second throw
Head	Head
Head	
Tail	
Tail	

(i) List all the possible outcomes:

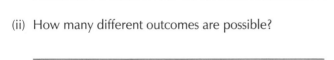

_____

_____

(ii) How many different outcomes are possible?

_____

Activity 3.8

List all the possible two-digit numbers that can be made from the digits 1, 2, 3 and 4, **using each digit only once** to make up your number.

1	2	3	4
12		31	
	24	34	

(i) How many outcomes are there? _____

(ii) How many digits does a bank card PIN (Personal Identification Number) have? _____

(iii) Explain how this makes the bank card more secure.

_____

_____

_____

(iv) The world's first ATM was installed in a branch of Barclays bank in north London in 1967. The inventor of the ATM, John Shepherd-Barron, wanted to have a six-digit PIN, but his wife, Caroline, was against this idea. What objection do you think she raised against a six-digit PIN?

_____

_____

_____

Activity 3.9

Two dice are thrown. Complete the sample space diagram below to show all the outcomes.

		Second die					
		1	2	3	4	5	6
First die	1		1, 2				
	2			2, 3			
	3						
	4						
	5						
	6	6, 1					6, 6

(i) How many outcomes are there? _____

(ii) What other method could you use to count the number of outcomes? _____

_____

(iii) How many outcomes have the same digits, for example (6, 6)? _____

(iv) Is the outcome (2, 3) the same as the outcome (3, 2)? _____

Explain your answer. _____

_____

Activity 3.10

A nine-sided spinner numbered 1 to 9 is spun and a coin is flipped.
Using the two-way table below, list all the outcomes.

		\multicolumn{9}{c}{**Spinner**}
		1	2	3	4	5	6	7	8	9
Coin	H		H2							
	T									T9

(i) How many outcomes are there? _____

(ii) How many outcomes have a tail and an odd number? _____

(iii) How many outcomes have a head and an even number? _____

Activity 3.11

Urn A contains tiles with the letters A, B, C, D and E on
them. Urn B contains tiles with the letters A, E, I, O and
U on them.

To win a competition, a student must draw out the same letter
from each pot, e.g. AA. The student has only one turn at this game.
Use the two-way table to list all the outcomes.

Urn A    Urn B

		\multicolumn{5}{c}{**Urn B**}
		A	E	I	O	U
Urn A	A					AU
	B					
	C					
	D		DE			
	E					

(i) How many outcomes are there? _____

(ii) How many winning outcomes are there? _____

(iii) What fraction of the total are winning outcomes? _____

(iv) Do you think that the student has a good chance of winning this game? _____

Give a reason for your answer. _____

_____

Activity 3.12

A coin is flipped three times. Use a tree diagram to show all the outcomes.

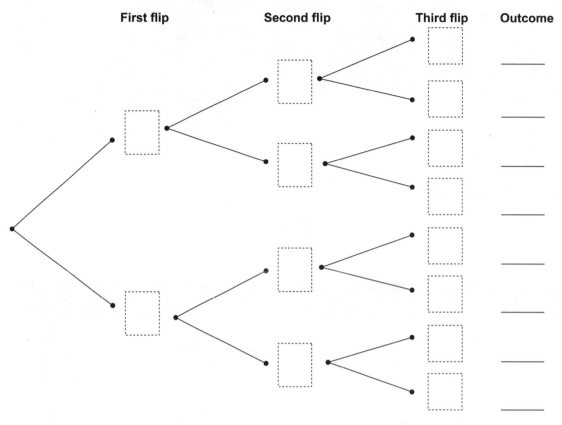

First flip	**Second flip**	**Third flip**	**Outcome**

(i) How many outcomes are there? _____

(ii) How many times does a tail appear in the outcomes? _____

(iii) How many outcomes have three heads? _____

Activity 3.13

A menu reads as follows:

Starter	Main	Dessert
Soup	Turkey	Ice-cream
Garlic bread	Ham	Cake
Salad	Beef	
	Lasagne	

(i) If a customer chooses one starter, one main and one dessert, how many different three-course meals do you think are possible?

_____

FUNDAMENTAL PRINCIPLE OF COUNTING

(ii) Use the tree diagram to show the number of outcomes. Some branches have been filled in for you:

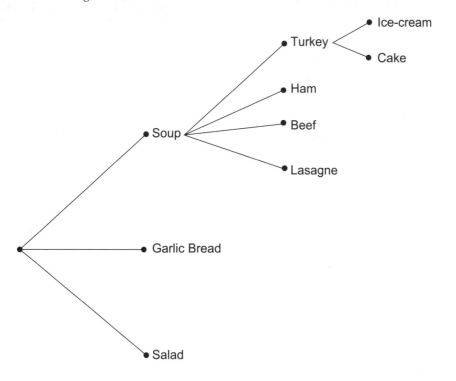

(iii) How many outcomes are there? _____

Is this the same as you thought in part (i)? _____

(iv) If the customer does not like lasagne, how many different three-course meals can she choose?

_____

Activity 3.14

In a restaurant, there are four choices for main course:
Fish, chicken, pasta or pizza.

There are three choices for dessert:
Cheesecake, ice-cream or apple tart.

(i) Use the Fundamental Principle of Counting to determine how many possible two-course meals you could have at this restaurant.

_____

(ii) List all the possible two-course meals you could have at this restaurant.

Activity 3.15

A student has two pairs of jeans (black or navy) and four tops (white, green, yellow or red).
How many different ways can this student dress, if we ignore all the other clothes?

Answer: There will be _____ different ways to dress.

In each case, colour in the various clothes. If you don't have colours, write the letter B (for black) or N (for navy) on the jeans, and W, G, Y or R (for white, green, yellow or red) on the tops.

Activity 3.16

Shane has an option of buying a car or a motorcycle.
There are six models of car available and two models of motorcycle.

(i) Which option has the most choice? _____

The car has a choice of two colours, while the motorcycle has a choice of three colours.

(ii) How many different models and colours of car could

Shane now buy? _____

(iii) How many different models and colours of

motorcycle could Shane now buy? _____

The car has a choice of three types of wheels, while the motorcycle has two types of wheel.

(iv) How many different cars could Shane now buy?

_____

(v) How many different motorcycles could Shane now

buy? _____

Integers

chapter 4

Activity 4.1

1. (i) Show the numbers in the yellow box on the numberline.

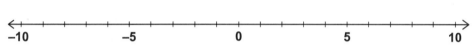

| −5 | 1 |
| −3 | |

(ii) Show the numbers in the blue box on the numberline.

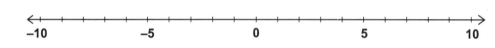

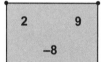

| 2 | 9 |
| −8 | |

(iii) Show the numbers in the orange box on the numberline.

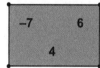

| −7 | 6 |
| 4 | |

(iv) Show the **opposites** of the numbers in the yellow box on the numberline.

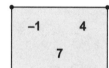

| −1 | 4 |
| 7 | |

(v) Show the **opposites** of the numbers in the blue box on the numberline.

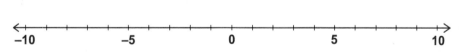

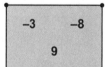

| −3 | −8 |
| 9 | |

(vi) Show the **opposites** of the numbers in the orange box on the numberline.

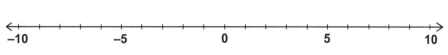

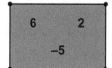

| 6 | 2 |
| −5 | |

2. (i) Write into the green circle the opposites of all the integers in the brown circle.

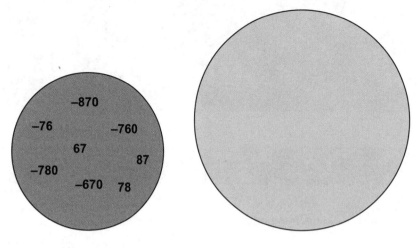

(ii) Starting with the smallest, write **in ascending order** all 16 integers in both circles (i.e. from the smallest number to the largest number).

3. (i) The orange circle below contains both positive and negative integers. In the green rectangle, write down all the **negative** integers from the circle. In the yellow rectangle, write down all the **positive** integers from the circle.

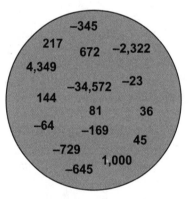

Negative   **Positive**

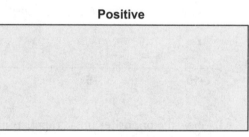

(ii) Take all 16 integers in the orange circle, and write in order from the largest to the smallest.

4. The temperature, measured in degrees Celsius, at midday was recorded every day for a week. The results are shown in the graph.

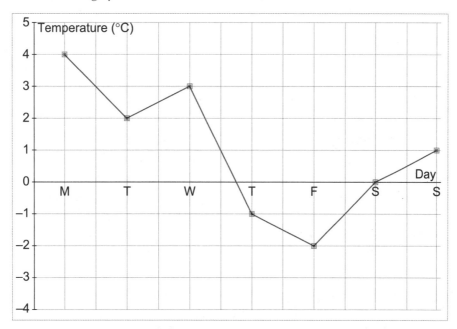

(i) What was the highest temperature recorded during the week?

(ii) What was the lowest temperature recorded during the week?

(iii) On what day was the first negative temperature recorded?

(iv) On what day was a temperature of 0° recorded?

(v) Order all the recorded temperatures, beginning with the smallest.

5. Do the crossnumber puzzle below.

Across

1. The opposite of the negative integer –238.

4. The largest even number that can be made from all the digits 1, 2, 3 and 4.

8. Reverse the digits of 4 across.

Down

2. The LCM of 17 and 22.

3. Reverse the digits of 7 down.

5. Its prime factorisation is $2^2 \times 3^2 \times 7^2$.

6. The square of 3 down.

7. The 11th prime number.

6. Match each number and symbol with the correct description in the table below. A number or symbol may only be used once as an answer.

24	–	–37	4	60	–5
–2	–9	3	>	–3	0

(i) A factor of 8 and also a factor of 12		(vii) The LCM of 5 and 12	
(ii) A positive number less than 6		(viii) A negative number less than –6	
(iii) A negative number greater than –5		(ix) The symbol for 'greater than'	
(iv) The sign that tells us a number is negative		(x) The sum of the two prime numbers that lie between 9 and 16	
(v) A negative number less than –2		(xi) An integer that is neither positive nor negative	
(vi) The opposite of the prime number that lies between 35 and 40		(xii) The opposite of the first odd prime number	

 Activity 4.2

Integers are made up of positive and negative whole numbers.
Zero is also an integer, although it is neither positive nor negative.

We can represent positive integers using green counters and negative integers using red counters. A green counter is the opposite to a red counter, as one is negative and the other is positive. Therefore, when we add a red counter to a green counter, they will eliminate each other.

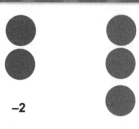

–2

+3

Example 1 Represent 4 in three different ways using red and green counters.

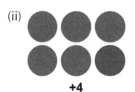

(i)   +4   (ii)   +4   (iii)   +4

1. By drawing red and green counters, represent each of the following numbers in three different ways. Remember that one red counter eliminates one green counter.

    (i) Represent the number **6** in three different ways.

1st way	2nd way	3rd way

INTEGERS

(ii) Represent the number **–8** in three different ways.

1st way	2nd way	3rd way

(iii) Represent the number **7** in three different ways.

1st way	2nd way	3rd way

2. What integer does each group of counters represent?

(i)
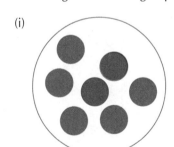
Integer = ⬚

(ii)
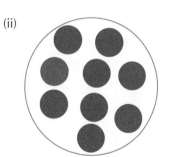
Integer = ⬚

(iii)
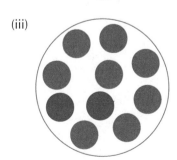
Integer = ⬚

(iv)
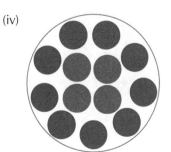
Integer = ⬚

Example 2 Use red and green counters to do the following sums:

(i) −3 − 4   (ii) 2 + 3   (iii) −5 + 3   (iv) 5 − 2

Solution

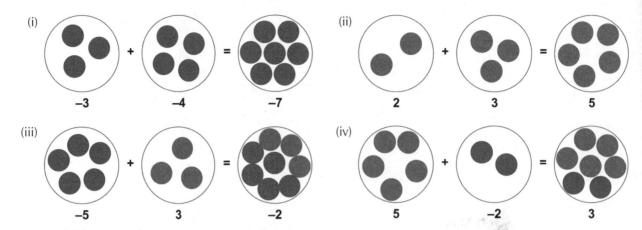

3. Use red and green counters to do the following sums:

(i) −3 − 2   (ii) 3 + 4   (iii) −4 + 3   (iv) 6 − 3

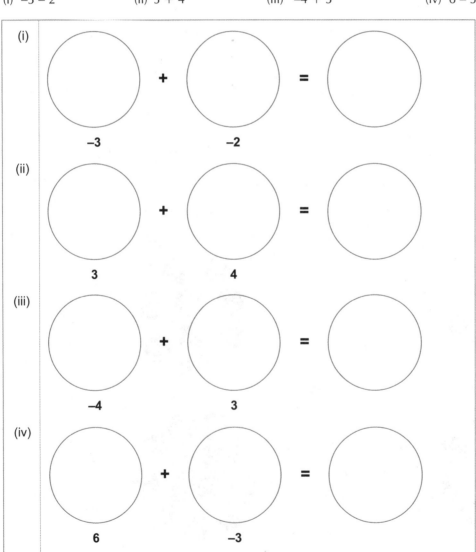

4. Answer **True** or **False** to each of the following statements.

If an answer is false, then give the correct statement.

(i) If I add a group of red counters to another group of red counters, the result will always be a group of red counters.

(ii) If I add a group of green counters to another group of green counters, the result will always be a group of green counters.

(iii) If I add a group of red counters to a group of green counters, the result will always be a group of red counters.

(iv) If I add a group of red counters to a group of green counters, and there are more green counters than red counters, the result will always be a group of red counters.

(v) If I add a group of red counters to a group of green counters, and there are more red counters than green counters, the result will always be a group of red counters.

5. Answer **True** or **False** to each of the following statements. If an answer is false, then give the correct statement.

(i) If I add a negative number to another negative number, the result will always be a negative number.

(ii) If I add a positive number to another positive number, the result will always be a positive number.

(iii) If I add a positive integer to a negative integer, the result will always be a negative integer.

(iv) A certain negative integer is further from zero on the numberline than a certain positive integer. If I add the positive integer to the negative integer, the result is a positive integer.

Example 3 – Subtraction

We often think of subtraction as 'taking away'. We can also use red and green counters to do subtraction.

Using counters, model the following subtraction questions and, hence, find the answer.

(i) 5 – (+3)   (ii) 2 – (+4)   (iii) 1 – (–4)

Solution

(i) 5 – (+3)

Here we are taking three green counters from five green counters.

5   take away 3 green =   **2**

Answer: 5 – (+3) = 2

(ii) 2 – (+4)

Here we do not have four green counters to take away, so we have to represent the two counters in a different way.

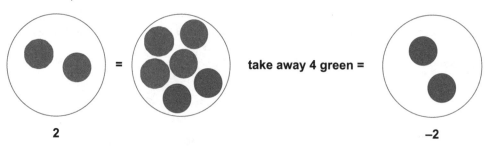

2   =   take away 4 green =   **–2**

Answer: 2 – (+4) = –2

(iii) 1 – (–4)

Now we do not have four red counters to take away, so we will have to represent one green counter in a way that includes four red counters.

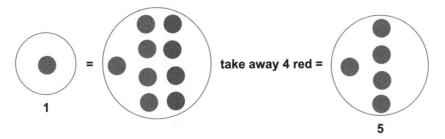

take away 4 red =

1

5

Answer: 1 – (–4) = 5

6. Using counters, model the following subtraction questions and, hence, find the answer.

(i) 4 – (+2) (iii) 2 – (–4)

(ii) 3 – (+4) (iv) –3 – (–2)

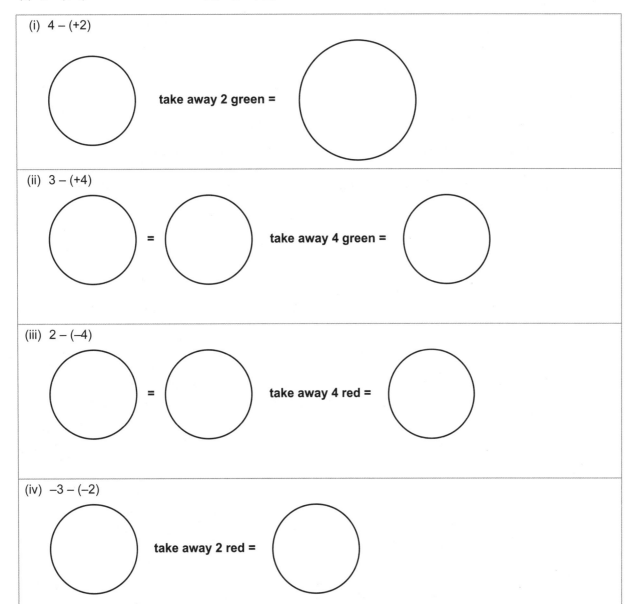

(i) 4 – (+2)

take away 2 green =

(ii) 3 – (+4)

= **take away 4 green =**

(iii) 2 – (–4)

= **take away 4 red =**

(iv) –3 – (–2)

take away 2 red =

INTEGERS

Example 4 – Multiplication

Evaluate the following products using the counter model.

(i) 3 × 2   (ii) 3 × –2   (iii) –2 × 3   (iv) –2 × –3

Solution

(i) 3 × 2 means three groups of two green counters.

  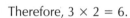

Therefore, 3 × 2 = 6.

(ii) 3 × –2 means three groups of two red counters.

Therefore 3 × –2 = –6.

(iii) –2 × 3

We need to use the commutative property to solve this question.

From part (ii): –2 × 3 = 3 × –2 = –6.

(iv) –2 × –3

–2 × –3 is the opposite of –2 × 3 (as they both add to give 0).

Therefore, as –2 × 3 = –6, then –2 × –3 = 6.

Answer **True** or **False** to each of the following statements. If an answer is false, then give the correct statement.

(i) If I multiply a negative number by another negative number, the result will always be a negative number.

(ii) If I multiply a positive number by another positive number, the result will always be a positive number.

(iii) If I multiply a positive integer by a negative integer, the result will always be a negative integer.

(iv) If I multiply a negative integer by a positive integer, the result will always be a negative integer.

INTEGERS

Rational Numbers

chapter 5

1. Shade or colour the fractions indicated on each of the given diagram:

(i)

$$\frac{1}{12}$$

(ii)

$$\frac{2}{12}$$

(iii)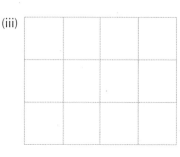

$$\frac{3}{12}$$

(iv)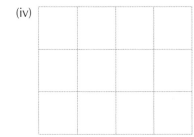

$$\frac{4}{12}$$

(v)

$$\frac{1}{12} + \frac{2}{12} + \frac{3}{12} + \frac{4}{12}$$

2. Shade or colour the fraction indicated on each of the given diagram:

(i)

$$\frac{1}{4}$$

(ii)

$$\frac{1}{3}$$

(iii)

$$\frac{5}{12}$$

(iv)

$$\frac{1}{4} + \frac{1}{3} + \frac{5}{12}$$

What is $\frac{1}{4} + \frac{1}{3} + \frac{5}{12}$?

3. Shade or colour the fractions indicated on each of the given diagrams:

(i)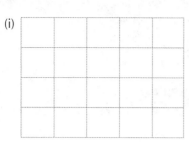

$$\frac{7}{20}$$

(ii)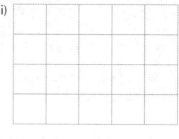

$$\frac{3}{20}$$

(iii)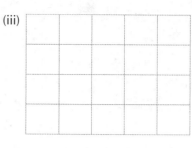

$$\frac{2}{20}$$

4. Shade or colour the fractions indicated on each of the given diagrams:

(i)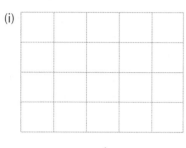

$$\frac{1}{4}$$

(ii)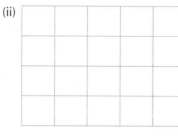

$$\frac{1}{2}$$

(iii)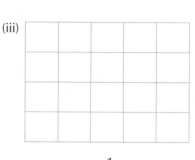

$$\frac{1}{5}$$

■ What is $\frac{1}{4} + \frac{1}{2} + \frac{1}{5}$?

5. (i) Using the diagram below, shade in two fractions that are equivalent to $\frac{1}{3}$.

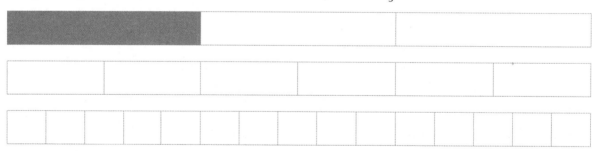

(ii) Using the diagram below, shade in two fractions that are equivalent to $\frac{1}{4}$.

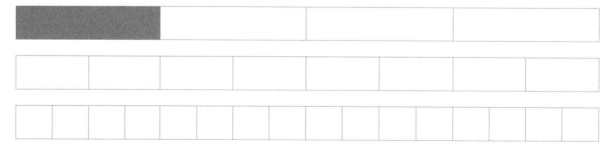

Activity 5.2

1. Using the fraction strips, evaluate these sums:

(i)

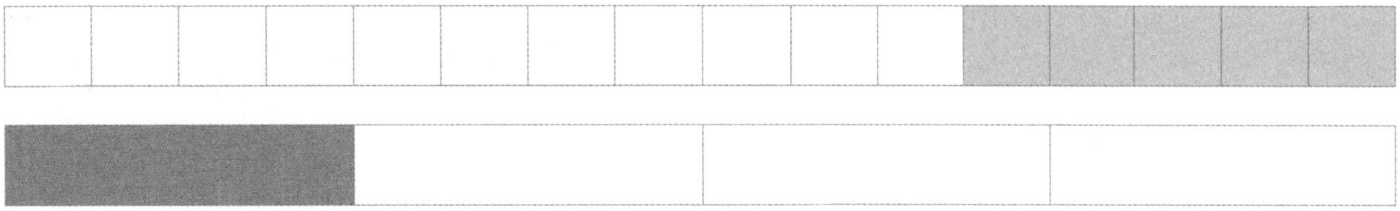

$$\frac{5}{16} + \frac{1}{4} =$$

(ii)

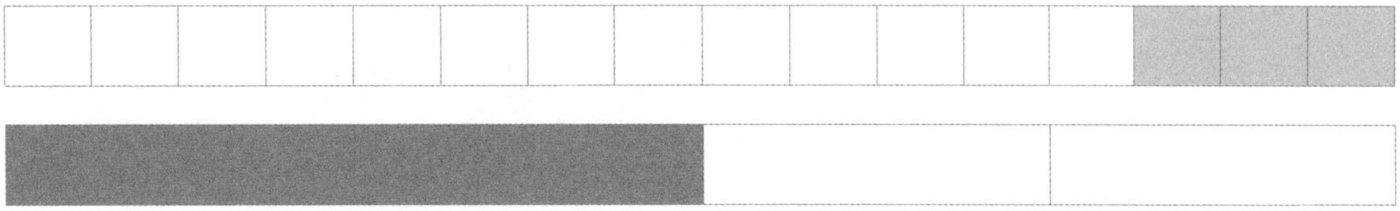

$$\frac{3}{16} + \frac{1}{2} =$$

(iii)

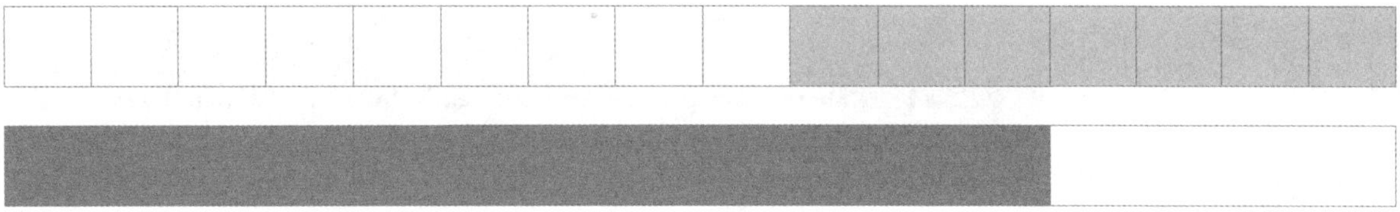

$$\frac{7}{16} + \frac{3}{4} =$$

2. Using the fraction strips, evaluate these sums:

(i)

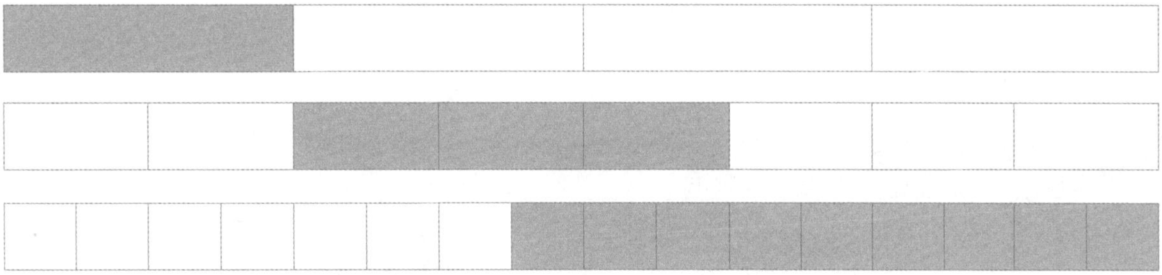

$$\frac{1}{4} + \frac{3}{8} + \frac{9}{16} =$$

(ii)

$$\frac{1}{2} + \frac{5}{8} + \frac{11}{16} =$$

(iii)

$$\frac{3}{4} + \frac{7}{8} + \frac{13}{16} =$$

Activity 5.3

1. Using the fraction strip below, find $\frac{2}{5} \times \frac{1}{2}$, i.e. $\frac{2}{5}$ of $\frac{1}{2}$.

$$\frac{2}{5} \times \frac{1}{2} =$$

2. Using the fraction strip below, find $\frac{2}{3} \times \frac{2}{3}$.

$$\frac{2}{3} \times \frac{2}{3} =$$

3. Using the fraction strip below, find $\frac{1}{2} \times \frac{1}{2}$.

$$\frac{1}{2} \times \frac{1}{2} =$$

4. You are given any two fractions, $\frac{\text{numerator}_1}{\text{denominator}_1}$ and $\frac{\text{numerator}_2}{\text{denominator}_2}$.

What is the product of these two fractions?

5. Marie and Jenny are playing a game. Marie multiplies the number 80 by a fraction from the disc below and says the answer. Jenny has to work out which fraction she used. Find out which fraction Marie used if she says:

$\frac{1}{4}$ $\frac{3}{5}$ $\frac{1}{5}$ $\frac{1}{2}$ $\frac{7}{20}$ $\frac{3}{10}$ $\frac{2}{5}$

Marie says	Fraction used
20	
16	
40	
24	
32	
28	
48	

Activity 5.4

1. Divide nine loaves equally among four people.

Show the divisions on the loaves above.

How many loaves does each person get?

Describe how you got this answer.

> [blank answer box]

2. Divide three loaves equally among eight people.

How much does each person get? [blank box]

Describe how you got this answer.

> [blank answer box]

3. Divide seven chocolate brownies equally among eight people.

How much does each person get? [blank box]

Describe how you got this answer.

> [blank answer box]

4. You have four bars of chocolate that you want to share among some of your friends.
You decide that $\frac{2}{5}$ of a bar should be enough for each person.
Use the fraction strips below to find out how many of your friends will get some chocolate.

Number of friends to get chocolate =

5. Leanne has four pizzas for a party. She decides that a serving should be $\frac{5}{8}$ of a pizza.
How many full servings can she get from the four pizzas?

Draw fraction strips to model the situation.

6 chapter Decimals and Percentages

% Activity 6.1

1. Using the diagrams, write the 'tenths' as 'hundredths'.

(i)
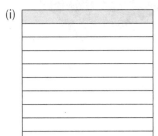
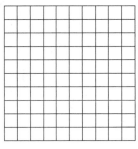

$$\frac{1}{10} = \frac{\boxed{10}}{100}$$

(iii)

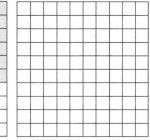

$$\frac{6}{10} = \frac{\boxed{60}}{100}$$

(ii)
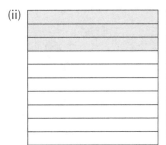
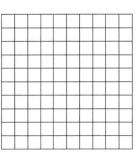

$$\frac{3}{10} = \frac{\boxed{30}}{100}$$

(iv)
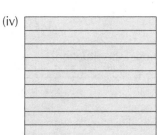
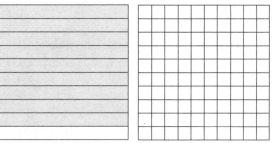

$$\frac{9}{10} = \frac{\boxed{90}}{100}$$

2. Using the diagrams below, do the additions:

(i)
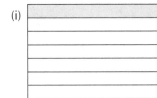
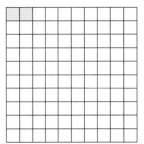

$$\frac{1}{10} + \frac{2}{100} = \boxed{12}$$

(ii)
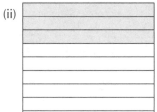
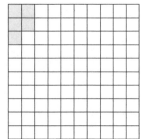

$$\frac{3}{10} + \frac{5}{100} = \boxed{35.}$$

(iii)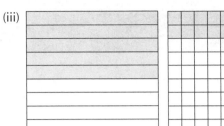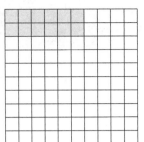

(iv)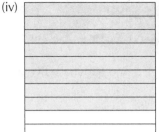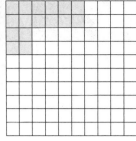

$\frac{5}{10} + \frac{12}{100} =$ 62.

$\frac{8}{10} + \frac{16}{100} =$ 96.

3. Can you spot a rule for adding tenths and hundredths? Explain in the box below.

4. Using your rule from Question 3, simplify $\frac{a}{10} + \frac{b}{100}$.

5. Simplify $2 + \frac{3}{10} + \frac{9}{100}$.

6. Question 5 should have simplified as $2\frac{39}{100}$. A simpler way of writing this fraction is 2.39. Similarly, $3\frac{456}{1,000}$ can be written as 3.456. This is called **writing the fraction as a decimal**. Write the following fractions as decimals:

Fraction	Decimal
$\frac{7}{10}$	0.40
$\frac{3}{100}$	0.3
$\frac{431}{1,000}$	0.431
$\frac{12}{10,000}$	0.012
$\frac{12,765}{100,000}$	0.012,765 .

1. (a) Use the digits 2, 3, 4, 5 and 6 to make five different five-digit numbers with:

   (i) One decimal place

   (ii) Two decimal places

   (iii) Three decimal places

You are not allowed to repeat digits in any of the numbers.

1 decimal place	2 decimal places	3 decimal places
3,246.5		
	452.63	
		23.654

(b) Complete the table below by rounding all the numbers above, to the nearest **whole number**.

3,247		
	453	
		24

2. In this question, we are allowed to use only the digits 0, 1 and 2 and the decimal point.

(a) 210 is one of the three-digit whole numbers that can be made from the digits 0, 1 and 2. Write down the three other three-digit whole numbers that can be made from these digits.

(b) Using all the digits 0, 1 and 2 and the decimal point, list the six three-digit numbers with two decimal places (one has already been done for you).

0.12					

(c) How many three-digit numbers with one decimal place can you make with the digits 0, 1 and 2? (Note: We do not consider '02.1' a three-digit number.)

3. (a) Complete the third column of the table by correcting **9567.45786**.

A	To one decimal place	
B	To the nearest whole number	
C	To one significant figure	10,000
D	To two decimal places	
E	To the nearest 100	
G	To seven significant figures	
H	To the nearest 10	
I	To five decimal places	
K	To eight significant figures	

(b) Complete the third column of the table by correcting **4,385.78243**.

L	To one decimal place	
M	To the nearest whole number	
N	To one significant figure	
O	To two decimal places	
R	To the nearest 100	
S	To seven significant figures	
T	To the nearest 10	
U	To five decimal places	
Y	To eight significant figures	

(c) In the tables in parts (a) and (b), a letter in Column 1 is associated with each number in Column 3. Using this information and the tables below, spell out the names of five famous people.
Column 2 contains the first name of the person and Column 4 contains the surname.

(i)

	First name		Surname
9,567		4,385.78	
9,567.5		9,567	
4,400		9,567.5	
9,567.5		4,386	
10,000		9,567.5	
9,567.4579			

(ii)

	First name		Surname
10,000		10,000	
9,570		4,385.78	
9,600		4,385.8	
4,400		9,600	
4,385.7824			
4,385.8			

(iii)

	First name		Surname
4,385.78243		9,567	
4,385.782		4,385.78	
9,567.5		4,385.8	
9,567.45786		4,390	
4,000			

(iv)

	First name		Surname
9,567.46		4,386	
9,567.5		9,567.45786	
4,000		4,000	
4,000		4,385.78	
9,567.45786		9,567.458	
		4,385.78243	
		9,600	

(v)

	First name		Surname
4,385.8		4,386	
9,567.45786		9,600	
4,385.78		4,385.782	
4,000		4,385.782	
9,600		9,567.45786	
4,385.8			

% Activity 6.3

1. What percentage of each of the following figures is shaded?

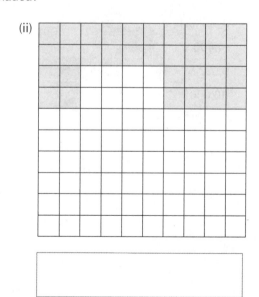

(i)

(ii)

(iii)

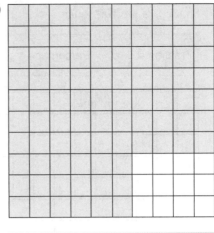

(iv)

2. By converting the fractions to percentages, do the following questions:

(i) Shade $\frac{1}{4}$ of the 100 square.

Fraction = $\frac{1}{4}$ Percentage =

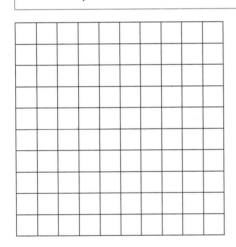

(iii) Shade $\frac{3}{4}$ of the 100 square.

Fraction = $\frac{3}{4}$ Percentage =

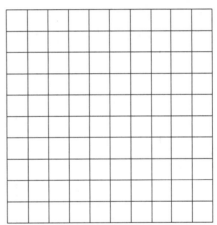

(ii) Shade $\frac{1}{2}$ of the 100 square.

Fraction = $\frac{1}{2}$ Percentage =

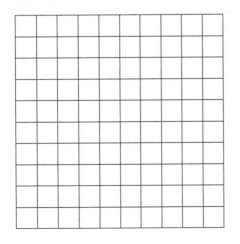

(iv) Shade $\frac{1}{5}$ of the 100 square.

Fraction = $\frac{1}{5}$ Percentage =

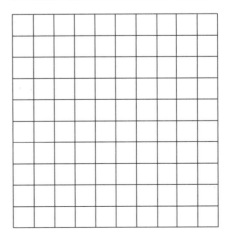

(v) Shade $\frac{2}{5}$ of the 100 square.

Fraction = $\frac{2}{5}$ Percentage =

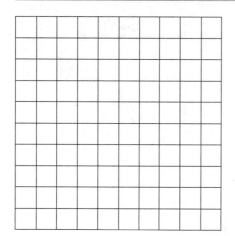

(vii) Shade $\frac{1}{10}$ of the 100 square.

Fraction = $\frac{1}{10}$ Percentage =

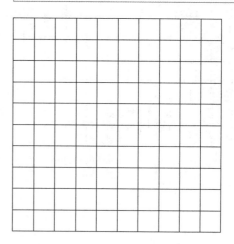

(vi) Shade $\frac{3}{5}$ of the 100 square.

Fraction = $\frac{3}{5}$ Percentage =

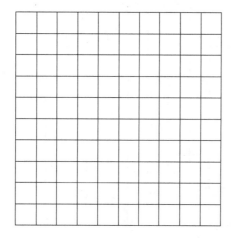

(viii) Shade $\frac{3}{10}$ of the 100 square.

Fraction = $\frac{3}{10}$ Percentage =

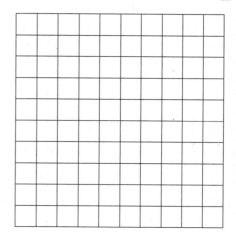

% Activity 6.4

If the red square represents 100%, write down the percentage that is shaded in the following diagrams:

(i)

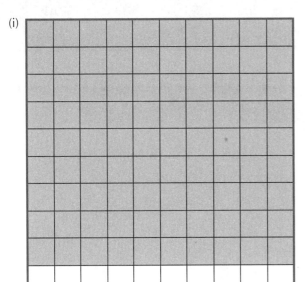

% Shaded =

(iii)

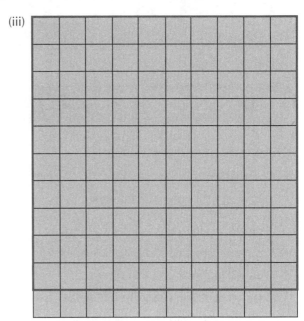

% Shaded =

(ii)

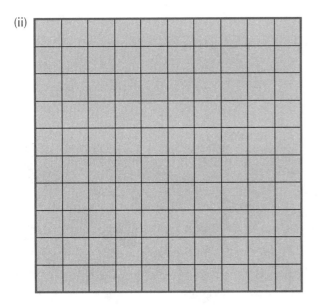

% Shaded =

(iv)

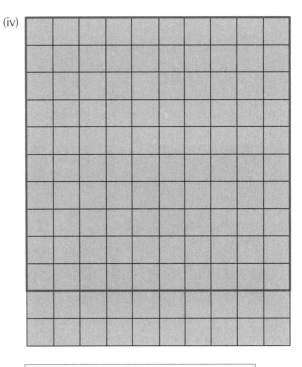

% Shaded =

7 chapter **Probability**

Activity 7.1

(i) Describe each of the following events as:

Impossible   Unlikely   Evens   Likely   Certain

Event	Probability
You will win the lotto.	Unlikely
You will score a goal in a football match.	
You will eat breakfast in the morning.	
You will be late to school next Monday.	
Given a crossword puzzle, you would be able to solve it.	
You will roll an 8 on a normal die.	
A flipped coin will land on a head.	
There will be 40 days in August.	
A new student to your class will be a boy.	
You will find a square with five sides.	
Ireland will win a gold medal at the next Summer Olympics.	
It will rain for the next 10 days.	
Ireland win the Eurovision Song Contest next year.	

(ii) Do you think your answers will be the same as your classmates' answers? _____

Explain why/why not. _____

_____

_____

Activity 7.2

(i) Match the phrase on the left-hand side with an appropriate word from the list below:

Impossible   Unlikely   Evens   Likely   Certain

Phrase	Probability
No chance	Impossible
Dead cert	
50–50	
Odds on favourite	
Pigs will fly	
Snowball's chance in hell	
A very good chance	
In all probability	
Million-to-one shot	

(ii) Can you or your partner think of any other phrases that are used to describe probability?

1. _____

2. _____

3. _____

(iii) Identify one problem with using the above phrases in describing probability.

_____

Activity 7.3

Place the letters A to J in the correct position on the probability scale below. 'A' has been done for you.

A	A tossed coin will land on a tail.
B	The day after Saturday will be Sunday.
C	It will snow this winter.
D	You will see a car on the road today.
E	There will be a full moon tonight.
F	You will visit the zoo this week.
G	You will throw a 1, 2 or 3 on a normal die.
H	You will pass your next maths exam.
I	You will draw a King from a deck of cards in a single pick.
J	You will live to be over 85 years old.

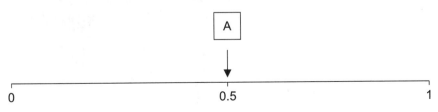

PROBABILITY

Activity 7.4

Place the letters K to V in the correct position on the probability scale below. 'K' has been done for you.

K	Almost certain
L	50% chance
M	Evens
O	3/4
P	0.25
Q	Very unilkely
R	1/4
S	Probable
T	Extremely likely
U	Never
V	Definite

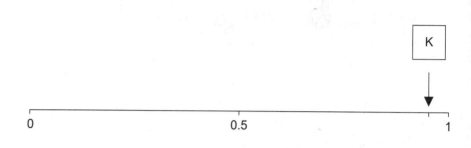

Activity 7.5

Make up your own event that corresponds to each of the arrows on the probability scale shown below.

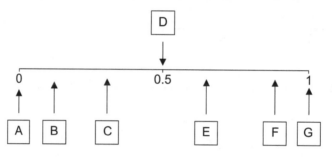

A	
B	
C	
D	
E	
F	
G	

Activity 7.6

A scientist keeps a daily record of how a series of experiments progressed over a month. She records the data using the following key (F = Experiment failed, S = Experiment succeeded):

F	S	S	S	S
S	F	S	F	S
F	S	S	S	S
S	S	F	F	S
F	S	S	S	S
F	F	S	F	F

PROBABILITY

(i) A day is picked at random. What is the experimental probability that on that day an experiment:

■ Failed _____

■ Did not fail _____

(ii) The scientist also noted that the experiment could have failed due to the very cold weather. Using this information and the table above, what month do you think the scientist was working in? _____

Activity 7.7

(i) A coin is tossed once.

Write down as a percentage what you think the probability is of getting a tail. _____

(ii) Flip a coin 20 times. In the table below, tally your results:

Result	Heads	Tails
Tally		
Total		
Fraction of total (relative frequency)	$\overline{20}$	$\overline{20}$
Percentage of total		

Is this what you predicted? _____

(iii) Add together the relative frequencies: _____

(iv) Now fill in this data from the whole class by adding up all the results throughout the class:

Result (from whole class)	Heads	Tails
Total number		
Fraction of total (relative frequency)		
Percentage of total (correct to 1 decimal place)		

Is this what you predicted? _____

(v) Add together the relative frequencies: _____

Which was closer to your prediction – your individual result or the class result?

_____

PROBABILITY

(i) A die is rolled 30 times.

What number do you think will appear the least number of times? _____

(ii) Roll a die 30 times. In the table below, tally your results:

Number on die	1	2	3	4	5	6
Tally						
Total						
Fraction of total	$\overline{30}$	$\overline{30}$	$\overline{30}$	$\overline{30}$	$\overline{30}$	$\overline{30}$
Percentage of total (1 d.p.)						

What number (if any) appeared the least? _____

Did this match your prediction? _____

> **Note: 1 d.p. = 1 decimal place**

(iii) If you added together all the relative frequencies, what answer would you expect? _____

Add up all the relative frequencies to check your answer. _____

(iv) Now fill out the table below with the number of 1's, 2's, etc. in the whole class:

Number on die	1	2	3	4	5	6
Total number in the whole class						
Total						
Fraction of total						
Percentage of total (1 d.p.)						

What number (if any) appeared the least in the whole class? _____

Did this match your prediction? _____

(v) Add together the relative frequencies for the class: _____

(vi) Compare your individual results with the class results.

Is there any noticeable difference? _____

Explain your answer. _____

_____

_____

Activity 7.9

(i) What suit in a normal deck of cards will appear most often: Club, Diamond, Heart or Spade?

_____

(ii) ■ Shuffle a deck of cards.

■ Select a card from the pack of cards, and record whether it is a Club, Diamond, Heart or Spade.

■ Return the card to the pack.

Do this 20 times. In the table below, tally your results:

Result	Tally	Total	Relative frequency	Percentage of total
Club				
Diamond				
Heart				
Spade				

Do these results match your prediction? _____

(iii) Now fill in this data from the whole class by adding up all the results throughout the class:

Result (from whole class)	Total	Relative frequency	Percentage of total (1 d.p.)
Club			
Diamond			
Heart			
Spade			

Do these results match your prediction? _____

(iv) Compare your individual results with the class results. Is there any noticeable difference? _____

Explain your answer. _____

_____

_____

Activity 7.10

Code breaking – An application of relative frequency

(i) What letter do you think is most commonly used in the English Language? ____________________

(ii) Analyse the following passage, and then fill in the table below. Some answers have been done for you.

> What are the two most common letters in the English language? Count the number of times each letter appears in this paragraph using tally marks. Then carefully fill in the table below.

Letter	Tally	Total		Letter	Tally	Total
a				n		
b	|||	3		o		
c	||||	4		p	||||	4
d				q		
e				r		
f	|||	3		s		
g				t		
h				u		
i				v		
j				w	|||	3
k	|	1		x		
l	𝍸 𝍸 |	11		y		
m				z		

According to the table, which letter appears most often? ____________________

Can we assume that this is true for any passage of the English language? Explain your answer.

____

____

____

(i) Throw a die 10 times. Use tally marks to record the number of times the number is odd or even.

Work out the relative frequencies for each event correct to two decimal places:

10 throws	Tally	Total	Relative frequency
Odd			
Even			

(ii) Repeat the experiment and record your results every 10 throws:

20 throws	Tally	Total	Relative frequency
Odd			
Even			

30 throws	Tally	Total	Relative frequency
Odd			
Even			

40 throws	Tally	Total	Relative frequency
Odd			
Even			

50 throws	Tally	Total	Relative frequency
Odd			
Even			

(iii) Using the graph paper below, plot the results of the relative frequency for getting an even number.

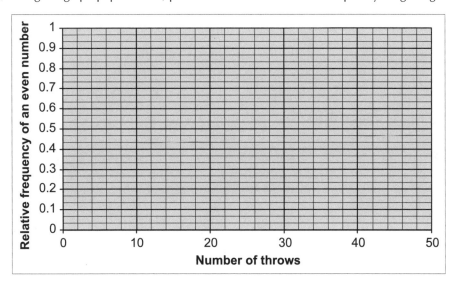

(iv) Does your data show that increasing the number of trials improves the accuracy of the relative frequency?

_____

_____

 **Activity 7.12**

This is a game for two players (Player 1 and Player 2). Player 1 picks heads, and Player 2 picks tails.

(i) Flip a coin **six times**. Keep a tally of the number of times Player 1 wins and the number of times Player 2 wins:

	Player 1 wins	Player 2 wins
Tally of number of times each player wins		
Total number of times each player wins		

(ii) Does this game appear to be fair? _____

Compare your results with those of your classmates: _____

(iii) Repeat the game, but this time flip the coin **12 times**:

	Player 1 wins	Player 2 wins
Tally of number of times each player wins		
Total number of times each player wins		

Do you think that increasing the number of trials affects how fair the game is? _____

_____

Explain your answer. _____

_____

Compare your results with those of your classmates. _____

(iv) Repeat the game but this time flip the coin **30 times**:

	Player 1 wins	Player 2 wins
Tally of number of times each player wins		
Total number of times each player wins		

What do you notice happens to the game as the number of trials increases?

_____

_____

This is a game for two players (called X and Y).

- ■ Roll a pair of dice.
- ■ Add the scores on each die to get the total.
- ■ Repeat this experiment until 40 rolls have been completed.

X wins if the total is 6, 7, 8 or 9.

Y wins if the total is 2, 3, 4, 5, 10, 11 or 12.

(i) Keep a tally of the number of times X wins and the number of times Y wins:

	X wins	**Y wins**
Tally of number of times each player wins		
Total number of times each player wins		

Is this game fair? _____

Give a reason for your answer. _____

_____

(ii) Can you change the rules so that the game would be fairer? If so, write down the new rules below:

X wins if the total is _____.

Y wins if the total is _____.

(iii) Play this new game. Roll the pair of dice 40 times. Keep a tally of the number of times X wins and the number of times Y wins.

	X wins	**Y wins**
Tally of number of times each player wins		
Total number of times each player wins		

Is your new game fair? _____

Explain your answer. _____

PROBABILITY

Activity 7.14

The following marbles are put in a bag.

A marble is chosen at random.

- What is the probability of picking a red marble? _____

- What is the probability of not picking a red marble? _____

- What is the probability of picking a yellow marble? _____

- What is the probability of picking a blue or green marble? _____

 Activity 7.15

The following coins are put into a box.

A coin is chosen at random.

- What is the probability of getting a 5c coin?

  _____

- What is the probability of **not** getting a 5c coin?

  _____

- What is the probability of getting a €2 or €1 coin?

  _____

 Activity 7.16

The following numbered tickets are put into a hat.

A ticket is chosen at random.

- What is the probability that it will be the ticket numbered 5?

  _____

- What is the probability that it will be a ticket showing a prime number?

  _____

- What is the probability that it will be an odd-numbered ticket?

  _____

- What is the probability that it will be an even-numbered ticket? _____

Activity 7.17

A group of boys and girls are picked for a team.

A picture of the team is shown opposite.

A student is chosen at random from the team.

- What is the probability that it will be a girl? _____

- What is the probability that it will **not** be a girl? _____

Activity 7.18

A bag of sweets is opened and the number of different coloured sweets is counted.

(i) In the table below, list the number of sweets of each different colour.

Red	Blue	Orange	Pink	Green

What is the total number of sweets in the bag? _____

(ii) One sweet is chosen at random from the bag. Write down the probability that the sweet picked is:

   (i) Red _____

  (ii) Pink _____

 (iii) Blue or pink _____

 (iv) Not red _____

  (v) Black _____

Activity 7.19

The cards shown are shuffled and placed face down on a table.

(i) A card is chosen at random. What is the probability that the card is:

- The Jack of Hearts _____

- The Ace of Hearts _____

- The Four of Hearts _____

- A card with a face _____

PROBABILITY

7

(ii) The picture cards are then removed (the Ace is not considered a picture card and counts as a 'one' for this question).

List the cards that are left:

(iii) A card is chosen at random from this new pack. What is the probability that the card is:

Even _____   Odd _____   7 or more _____   3 or less _____

Activity 7.20

A fair coin is flipped.

(i) What is the probability of getting a head? _____

(ii) Flip a coin 50 times, and after every 10 flips record your results in the table below. Fill in the tally, number of heads obtained, the relative frequency and the theoretical probability for 10, 20, 30, 40 and 50 flips of a coin.

Number of times coin flipped	Tally	Number of heads obtained	Relative frequency of getting a head	Theoretical probability
10		___ out of 10 flips	$\frac{}{10}$ =	$\frac{}{10}$
20		___ out of 20 flips	$\frac{}{20}$ =	$\frac{}{20}$
30		___ out of 30 flips	$\frac{}{30}$ =	$\frac{}{30}$
40		___ out of 40 flips	$\frac{}{40}$ =	$\frac{}{40}$
50		___ out of 50 flips	$\frac{}{50}$ =	$\frac{}{50}$

How many heads did you get? _____

(iii) What is the relative frequency of a getting a head, based on your results for 50 flips? _____

Does this match the theoretical probability? _____

If not, why? _____

_____

PROBABILITY

Activity 7.21

In Column B, fill in the probability of each event for rolling a die once. Add the probabilities together and fill in the total:

A	B	C	D	E	F
Number on die	Probability (single roll)	Tally	Relative frequency from 12 die rolls	Tally	Relative frequency from 60 die rolls
1	$\frac{1}{6}$				
2					
3					
4					
5					
6					
Total					

- Roll the die 12 times, record the tally in column C and fill in the relative frequency in Column D.

- Add the relative frequencies together. What do you notice? _____

_____

- Do the relative frequencies match the probabilities? _____

- Roll the die 60 times, record the tally in column E and fill in the relative frequencies in Column F.

- Add the relative frequencies together. What do you notice? _____

_____

- Do these results more closely match the probabilities in Column B? _____

  If so, explain why. _____

_____

_____

 Activity 7.22

(i) Colour in the sectors in the spinners as instructed:

Spinner 1: Two red, two green, two blue

Spinner 2: One red, two blue, three green

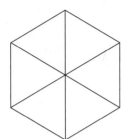

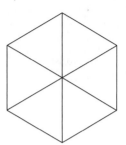

(ii) Complete the following table:

	Spinner 1	Spinner 2
Expected frequency of red (1 spin)		
Expected frequency of blue (1 spin)		
Expected frequency of green (1 spin)		
Expected frequency of red (60 spins)		
Expected frequency of blue (240 spins)		
Expected frequency of green (600 spins)		

Activity 7.23

A die is rolled 30 times.

(i) Write in the expected frequency for each die roll in the table below.

Number on die	Expected frequency	Actual frequency
1		
2		
3		
4		
5		
6		

(ii) Roll a die 30 times and record your results in the 'Actual Frequency' column.

Is the expected frequency equal to the actual frequency? _____

Give a reason for any differences. _____

_____

_____

PROBABILITY

Activity 7.24

(i) List all the Presidents of Ireland since 1938.

1.	5.
2.	6.
3.	7.
4.	8.

(ii) How many are:

■ Male _____

■ Female _____

(iii) Looking at the data you collected, what do you think is the probability that the next president will be:

■ Male _____

■ Female _____

Activity 7.25

The fair spinner shown is spun.

(i) List all the possible outcomes:

1	2	3	4	5	6	7	8	9	10
11	12	13	14	15	16	17	18	19	20

How many outcomes are possible? _20_

(ii) List the outcomes in which the spinner will land on an even number:

2	4	6	8	10	12	14	16	18	20

How many outcomes are there in this case? _10_

Probability of getting an even number = $\dfrac{1}{2}$

(iii) List the outcomes where the spinner will land on an odd number:

1	3	5	7	9	11	13	15	17	19

How many outcomes are there in this case? ___10___

Probability of getting an odd number = $\boxed{^1/_2}$

(iv) Is there an easier way to calculate the probability of getting an odd number? ___Yes_____

Explain. __Find the relative frequency_____

_____

_____

(v) List the outcomes where the spinner will land on a prime number:

2	3	5	7	11	13	17	19

How many outcomes are there in this case? ___8___

Probability of getting a prime number = $\boxed{^2/_5}$

What would be the probability of **not** getting a prime number? $\boxed{^3/_5}$

A fair coin is flipped and an unbiased die is rolled.

(i) Fill in the sample space diagram below using head (H) and tail (T) for the coin and the numbers 1 to 6 for the die.

		Die					
		1	2	3	4	5	6
Coin	H	H1	H2	H3	H4	H5	H6
	T	T1	T2	T3	T4	T5	T6

(ii) How many different outcomes are possible? ___12_____

(iii) How many outcomes show a head and a one? ___1_____

What is the probability of getting a head and a one? ___$^1/_{12}$_____

(iv) How many outcomes will show a tail and a 6? ___1_____

What is the probability of getting a tail and a 6? ___$^1/_{12}$_____

(v) How many outcomes will show a tail and an even number? ___3_____

What is the probability of getting a tail and an even number? ___$^1/_4$_____

(vi) How many outcomes will show a head and an odd number? ___3_____

What is the probability of getting a head and an odd number? ___$^1/_4$_____

Activity 7.27

Spinner A has the numbers 2, 7, 9 and 11 on it. Spinner B has the numbers 3, 4, 5 and 6 on it.

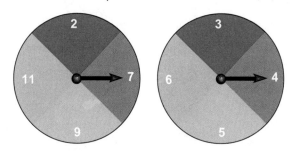

(i) The two spinners are spun and the score from each spinner is added together. Complete the table below to show all the possible scores. Two have been done for you.

		Spinner B			
		3	4	5	6
Spinner A	2	5	6	7	8
	7	10	11	12	13
	9	12	13	14	15
	11	14	15	16	17

(ii) How many outcomes are possible? __16__

(iii) How many outcomes are odd? ____ . __8__

Find the probability of getting an odd number. __8/16__

(iv) How many outcomes are even? __8__

Find the probability of getting an even number. __8/16__

(v) How many outcomes are greater than 13? __4__

Find the probability of getting a score greater than 13. __1/4__

(vi) How many outcomes are multiples of 5? __4__

Find the probability of getting a score that is a multiple of 5. __1/4__

Find the probability of getting a score that is **not** a multiple of 5. __3/4__

PROBABILITY

A fair coin is flipped twice.

(i) Fill in all the possible outcomes using the tree diagram below:

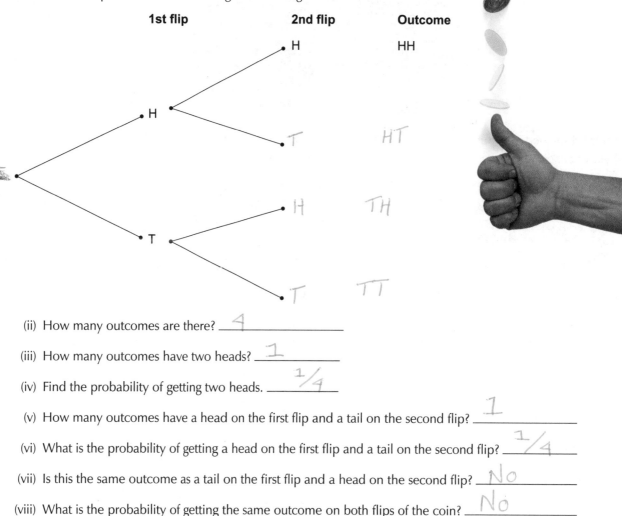

1st flip	2nd flip	Outcome
H	H	HH
	T	HT
T	H	TH
	T	TT

PROBABILITY

(ii) How many outcomes are there? _____4_____

(iii) How many outcomes have two heads? _____1_____

(iv) Find the probability of getting two heads. _____1/4_____

(v) How many outcomes have a head on the first flip and a tail on the second flip? _____1_____

(vi) What is the probability of getting a head on the first flip and a tail on the second flip? _____1/4_____

(vii) Is this the same outcome as a tail on the first flip and a head on the second flip? _____No_____

(viii) What is the probability of getting the same outcome on both flips of the coin? _____No_____

Number Patterns

 Activity 8.1

A repeating pattern for a tiled border is shown below.

(i) Fill in the following table:

Tile	Colour	Tile	Colour	Tile	Colour	Tile	Colour
1		11		21		31	
2		12		22		32	
3		13		23		33	
4		14		24		34	
5		15		25		35	
6		16		26		36	
7		17		27		37	
8		18		28		38	
9		19		29		39	
10		20		30		40	

(ii) What colour is the: 20th tile: _____

26th tile: _____

33rd tile: _____

39th tile: _____

50th tile: _____

(iii) Do you notice any rules that would help you in finding the colour of any given tile?

Rule 1: _____

Rule 2: _____

By filling in the red boxes for each sequence, find the next three terms.

(i) Start term = _____

Difference between each term = _____

1st Term	2nd Term	3rd Term	4th Term	5th Term	6th Term
5	**11**	**17**			

What do you notice about the difference between each term?

_____

Rule: Start with _____ and _____ every term.

(ii) Start term = _____

Difference between each term = _____

1st Term	2nd Term	3rd Term	4th Term	5th Term	6th Term
12	**22**	**32**			

Rule: Start with _____ and _____ every term.

(iii) Start term = _____

Difference between each term = _____

1st Term	2nd Term	3rd Term	4th Term	5th Term	6th Term
18	**25**	**32**			

Rule: Start with _____ and _____ every term.

(iv) Start term = _____

Difference between each term = _____

1st Term	2nd Term	3rd Term	4th Term	5th Term	6th Term
8	**3**	**−2**			

Rule: Start with _____ and _____ every term.

NUMBER PATTERNS

Activity 8.3

Examine the sequence 2, 5, 8, 11, 14...

Follow the given steps to help find T_n (the general term).

Common difference = ⬚

Term number	Difference × term number				
T_1	3	×	1	=	3
T_2	3	×	2	=	6
T_3	___	×	3	=	___
T_4	___	×	___	=	___
T_5	___	×	___	=	___

Term number		Term value
T_1	3 – ___ = 2	2
T_2	6 – ___ = 5	5
T_3	___ – ___ = 8	8
T_4	___ – ___ = 11	11
T_5	___ – ___ = 14	14

General term	
T_n	( ) × n – ( ) =

$T_n =$ ___

Activity 8.4

By filling in the red and blue boxes for each quadratic sequence, find the next three terms.

(i)

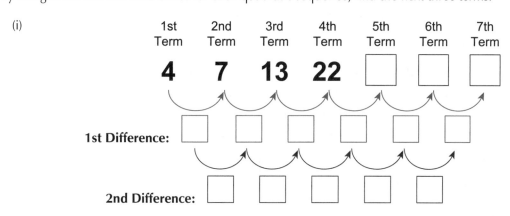

Start term = _____

What do you notice about the first difference between each term?

_____

Second difference between each term = _____

(ii)

	1st Term	2nd Term	3rd Term	4th Term	5th Term	6th Term	7th Term
	15	**20**	**34**	**57**	☐	☐	☐

1st Difference: ☐ ☐ ☐ ☐ ☐ ☐

2nd Difference: ☐ ☐ ☐ ☐ ☐

Start term = _____

Second difference between each term = _____

(iii)

	1st Term	2nd Term	3rd Term	4th Term	5th Term	6th Term	7th Term
	1	**7**	**22**	**46**	☐	☐	☐

1st Difference: ☐ ☐ ☐ ☐ ☐ ☐

2nd Difference: ☐ ☐ ☐ ☐ ☐

Start term = _____

Second difference between each term = _____

(iv)

	1st Term	2nd Term	3rd Term	4th Term	5th Term	6th Term	7th Term
	1	**5**	**6**	**4**	☐	☐	☐

1st Difference: ☐ ☐ ☐ ☐ ☐ ☐

2nd Difference: ☐ ☐ ☐ ☐ ☐

Start term = _____

Second difference between each term = _____

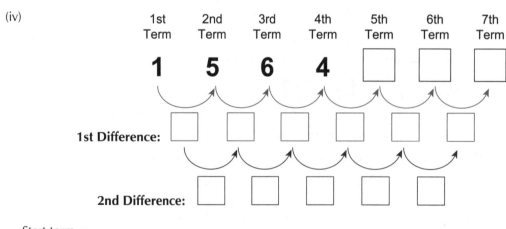

NUMBER PATTERNS

(i) Consider the following sequence:

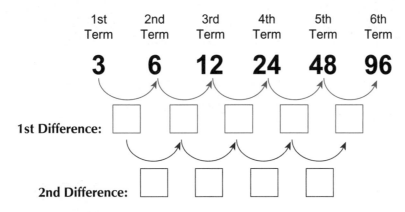

Start term = _____

What do you notice about the first difference between each term?

_____

What do you notice about the second difference between each term?

_____

Can you think of another way to get from term to term?

_____

(ii) By filling in the green boxes for each exponential sequence, find the next three terms.

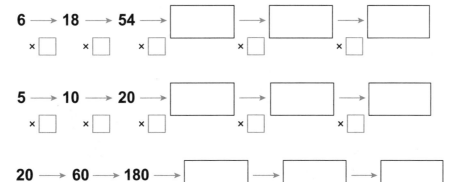

Algebra: An Introduction

x^2 Activity 9.1

If $a = 4$, $b = 5$, $c = 3$ and $d = 1$, complete the following number crossword.
Number 1 Across has been done for you.

	Across		Down
1	$5a = 5(4) = 20$	**1**	$4b + 1$
2	$4c$	**3**	$3a$
3	$2b + a$	**4**	$2a + 4b$
4	$4a + b + d$	**5**	$6c + a + 2d$
5	$7c + b$	**6**	$3b - 2d$
7	$6a - d$	**8**	$8b + 2c - 2d$
8	$6a + 5b - d$		

x^2 Activity 9.2

If $a = 10$, $b = 5$, $c = -3$ and $d = -2$, complete the following number crossword.
Number 1 Down has been done for you.

	Across		Down
1	$6a + 8b + 2$	**1**	$b^2 + 3c = (5)^2 + 3(-3) = 25 - 9 = 16$
3	$ab + 1$	**2**	$a + b - 4c + d$
5	$3a + d$	**4**	$-4c$
6	$2c^2$	**7**	$(-c)^4 - 2c$
8	$c^2(a + d)$	**9**	$-11d$
12	$b - 2ac$	**10**	$a^2 + 6c - 1$
13	$d^3 + 2a - c$	**11**	$(a + c)b$
15	$(a + d)(-2c)$	**12**	$(cd)a^2 + b$
16	$(a - d)d^2$	**14**	$ab + cd - 1$
18	$(c^2 + d)^2 + (b + d)$	**17**	$4b - 9c + 3$
20	$4c^2 + 2b + d$	**19**	$-bc - 3c$
22	abc^2	**21**	$4b^2 - 2a - 2d$

(i) Complete the following table (the first one has been done for you):

4 apples + 2 apples	6 apples
1 apple + 2 apples	
4 oranges + 3 oranges	
2 oranges + 1 orange + 2 apples	
2 apples − 1 orange − 2 apples	
3 boys + 2 girls − 1 boy	
4 dogs − 2 cats − 1 dog + 3 cats	

(ii) Fill in the following table:

$4x + 2x$	$(x + x + x + x) + (x + x)$	$= 6x$
$5a + 3a$		
$3p + 3p$		
$3y − 2y$	$(y + y + y) − (y + y)$	
$3x + 2x + x$		
$5y + y + y$		
$2x^2 + 3x^2$	$(x^2 + x^2) + (x^2 + x^2 + x^2)$	
$3x^2 − 3x^2$		
$x^2 + x^2 + x$		

x^2 Activity 9.4

Consider the following magic square. In a magic square, the sums of all rows, columns or diagonals are equal:

			Total
12x	14x	4x	30x
2x	10x	18x	30x
16x	6x	8x	30x
Total 30x	30x	30x	30x

The 'magic number' is 30x.

Complete the following magic squares.

(i)

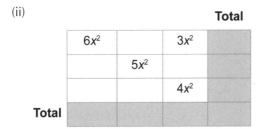

(iii)

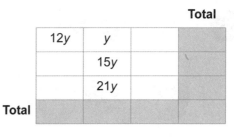

(ii)

6x²		3x²	
	5x²		
		4x²	
Total			

(iv)

12y	y		
	15y		
	21y		
Total			

x^2 Activity 9.5

Using the table below, simplify the following:

	Number by number	Variable by variable	Answer
$4a^2 \times 3a$	$4 \times 3 = 12$	$a \times a \times a = a^3$	$12a^3$
$2x \times 3x$			
$(5p)(2p)$			
$(3y^2)(y)$			
$(8b)(-2b^2)$			
$(-5a^3)(4a)$			
$(-2p^2)(-2p)$			
$(5xy)(2xy)$			
$(ab)(3abc)$			
$(7pr)(3rp^2)$			
$(4x^2)(-xy^2)$			
$(-b^2c)(-bc^3)$			

x^2 Activity 9.6

Using the boxes, simplify the following (the first one has been done for you):

(i) $6(x + 1) =$

	x	$+1$
6	$6x$	$+6$

$= 6x + 6$

(v) $4(x + 2y - 3) =$

	x	$+2y$	$- 3$
4			

$=$ _____

(ii) $10(x - 2) =$

	x	-2
10		

$=$ _____

(vi) $5(a - 3b - c) =$

$=$ _____

(iii) $3(4x + 5) =$

	$4x$	$+5$
3		

$=$ _____

(vii) $-(3x - 5y - 1) =$

$=$ _____

(iv) $-2(3a - 3) =$

	$3a$	-3
-2		

$=$ _____

x^2 Activity 9.7

Using the boxes, simplify the following (the first one has been done for you):

(i) $2x(x + 4) =$

	x	$+4$
$2x$	$2x^2$	$8x$

$= 2x^2 + 8x$

(v) $3a(2a - 4b + 1) =$

	$2a$	$- 4b$	$+1$
$3a$			

$=$ _____

(ii) $3x(x - 1) =$

	x	-1
$3x$		

$=$ _____

(vi) $3x(2x - 2y - 4z) =$

$=$ _____

(iii) $2x(3x + 2) =$

	$3x$	$+2$
$2x$		

$=$ _____

(vii) $-2x(-x - 4y - 5) =$

$=$ _____

(iv) $-5x(2x - 3) =$

	$2x$	-3
$-5x$		

$=$ _____

x^2 Activity 9.8

Using the boxes, simplify the following (the first one has been done for you):

(i) $(x + 1)(x + 2) =$

	x	+2	x^2 terms	x terms	Number
x	x^2	+2x	x^2	+2x	
+1	+1x	+2		+1x	+2
		Answer =	x^2	+3x	+2

(ii) $(x + 3)(x + 4) =$

	x	+4	x^2 terms	x terms	Number
x					
+3					
		Answer =			

(iii) $(x - 1)(x - 5) =$

	x	–5	x^2 terms	x terms	Number
x					
–1					
		Answer =			

(iv) $(x - 7)(x + 2) =$

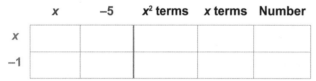

		x^2 terms	x terms	Number
	Answer =			

(v) $(x - 4)(x + 4) =$

		x^2 terms	x terms	Number
	Answer =			

(vi) $(x - 3)(x - 3) =$

		x^2 terms	x terms	Number
	Answer =			

Algebra: Solving Linear Equations

x^2 Activity 10.1

Complete the table. The first row has been done for you.

	Equation	Solve
9 + ? = 19	9 + x = 19	x = 10
7 − ? = 2		
? + 8 = 12		
3 + 12 − ? = 4		
−10 + ? = −7		
−1 − ? = −5		
12 × ? = 36		
? × 5 = 20		
? × −1 = 4		
−3 × ? = −45		
2 × 5 × ? = 60		
? × 4 × 5 = 180		
12 ÷ ? = 4		
? ÷ 10 = 4		

Activity 10.2

Find the cost of each single item:

1.

= _____

2.

= _____

3.

= _____

4.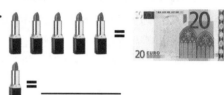

= _____

5.

= _____

6.

= _____

Activity 10.3

Find the cost of each single item:

1.  **+** **=**

 = _____

 = _____

2.

3.

4.

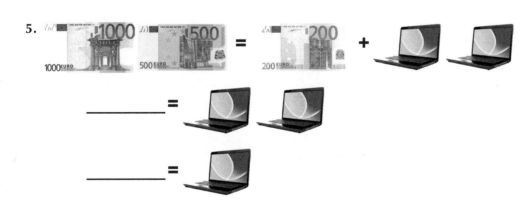

5.

Geometry I

chapter

Activity 11.1

On the plane below, identify and name:

(i) Two lines

(ii) Two rays

(iii) Two line segments

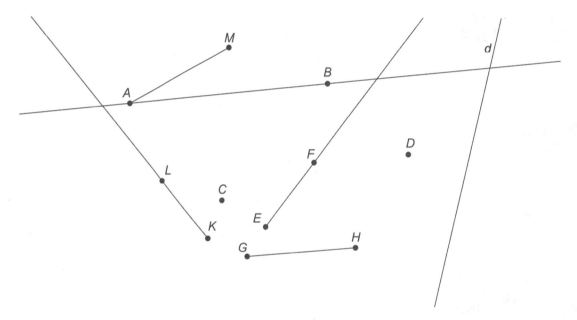

| (i) Lines | AB | d ✓ |

| (ii) Rays | [EF | [KL ✓ |

| (iii) Line segments | |AM| | |GH| ✓ |

1. On the plane below draw the following:

(i)   A line *AB* ✓

(ii) A line *CD* ✓

(iii) A ray *[AG* ✓

(iv) A ray *[BE* ✓

(v)   A half-line *[EF* (Ray) ✓

(vi) A line segment *[GH]* ✓

(vii) A line segment *[BD]* ✓

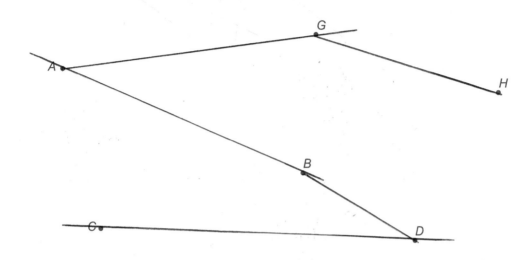

2. (i) Find $|GH|$ = __5·5cm__ ✓ and $|DB|$ = __3·5cm__ ✓ .

   (ii) Is $|HG|$ = $|GH|$? __Yes__ ✓

      Give a reason for your answer. __because the length from G to H is 5·5cm and |HG| is also 5·5cm__

3. Can you measure the ray *[AG*? __No__ ✓

   Explain. __because a ray has only one endpoint so it can go on forever__

4. Name three points on the given plane that are collinear.

> A, B, D ✗   G, B, E

Activity 11.3

(i) Given the points *D*, *E*, *F* and *G*, draw all the possible line segments that connect any two of the given points.

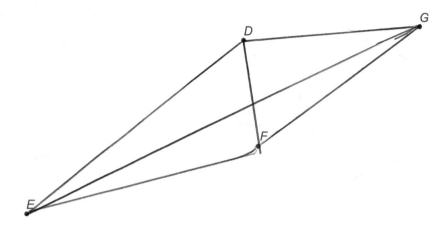

(ii) How many line segments did you draw? ___6___ ✓

(iii) Measure all the line segments to the nearest millimetre.
The first one has been done for you:

|*DE*| = 75 mm

Activity 11.4

1. (i) How many degrees are there in a quarter-turn? ___90°___ ✓

    (ii) This type of angle is called a ___right___ ✓ angle.

    (iii) Draw what this angle would look like without using a protractor.

    (iv) What symbol denotes this type of angle? ___┐___ ✓

2. (i) How many degrees are there in a half-turn? ___180°___ ✓

    (ii) This type of angle is called a ___straight___ ✓ angle.

    (iii) Draw what this angle would look like without using a protractor.

3. (i) How many degrees are there in a three-quarter turn? ___270°___ ✓

    (ii) Draw what this type of angle would look like without using a protractor.

4. (i) How many degrees are there in a full turn? ___360°___ ✓

    (ii) Draw what this type of angle would look like without using a protractor.

Activity 11.5

1. Draw an acute angle. Label it as ∠ABC.
   An acute angle can have a degree measure between 0° and <u>90°</u>.

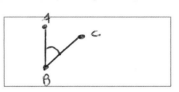

2. Draw an obtuse angle. Label it as ∠XYZ.
   An obtuse angle can have a degree measure between

   <u>90°</u> and <u>180°</u>.

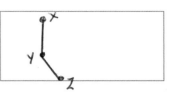

3. Draw a reflex angle. Label it as angle α.
   A reflex angle can have a degree measure between

   <u>180°</u> and <u>270°</u>.

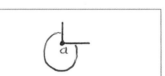

4. Draw an ordinary angle. Label it as angle 1.
   An ordinary angle can have a degree measure between

   <u>0°</u> and <u>180°</u>.

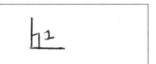

Activity 11.6

Use two different ways to name each of the following angles. The first one has been done for you.

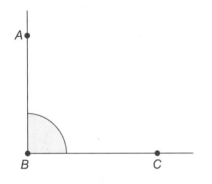

(i) ∠ABC	(ii) ∠B

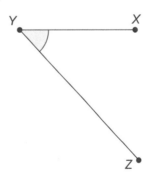

(i) ∠XYZ	(ii) ∠Y

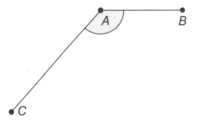

(i) ∠CAB	(ii) ∠A

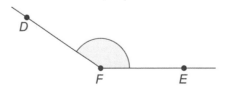

(i) ∠DFE	(ii) ∠F

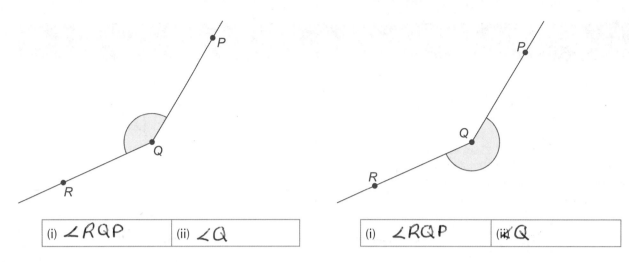

(i) ∠RQP	(ii) ∠Q

(i) ∠RQP	(ii) ∠Q

What extra information must you give to tell the difference between the last two angles?

_____

Activity 11.7

Name the angle shown in each of the following diagrams. The first one is done for you.

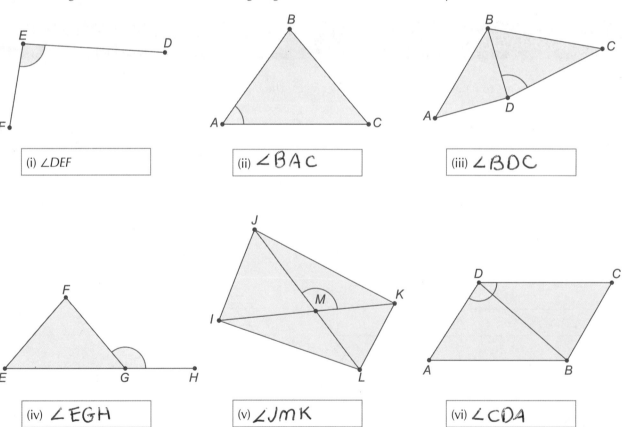

(i) ∠DEF

(ii) ∠BAC

(iii) ∠BDC

(iv) ∠EGH

(v) ∠JMK

(vi) ∠CDA

Using a protractor, name and measure the following angles:

(i)
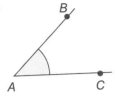

Name: ∠BAC

Measure: 50°

(ii)
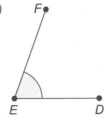

Name: ∠FED

Measure: 70°

(iii)
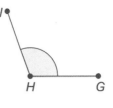

Name: ∠IHG

Measure: 110°

(iv)
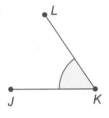

Name: ∠LKJ

Measure: 55°

(v)
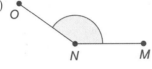

Name: ∠ONM

Measure: 145°

(vi)
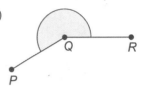

Name: ∠PQR

Measure: 210°

(vii)
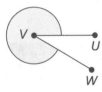

Name: ∠UVW

Measure: 330°

(viii)
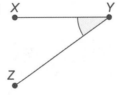

Name: ∠XYZ

Measure: 35°

(ix)
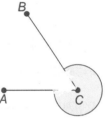

Name: ∠BCA

Measure: 305°

(x)
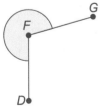

Name: ∠GFO

Measure: 255°

Activity 11.9

Without using a protractor, estimate each of the following angles.
When you have estimated all the angles, check your answers using a protractor.

(i)

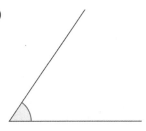

Estimation: 70°

Actual: 55°

(iii)

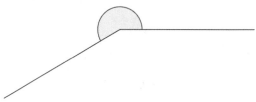

Estimation: 210

Actual: 210°

(ii)

Estimation: 110°

Actual: 150°

(iv)

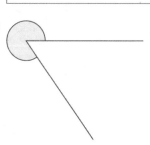

Estimation: 300°

Actual: 305°

 Activity 11.10

1. (i) Draw two lines that are perpendicular to each other.

(ii) What is the symbol we use to show that these two lines are perpendicular? | ⊓ |

2. (i) Draw two lines that are parallel to each other.

_____

_____

(ii) What is the symbol we use to show that these two lines are parallel? | ⊥ |

3. Identify parallel lines and perpendicular lines in your classroom.

> Walls
> Table
> Chair
> Book

Activity 11.11

In the following diagrams, identify all the lines that are perpendicular or parallel to each other.

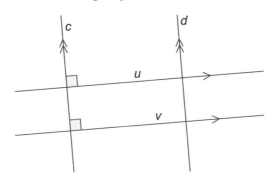

> $c \perp u$ $d \perp u$
>
> $c // d$ $c \perp v$
>
> $u // v$ $d \perp v$

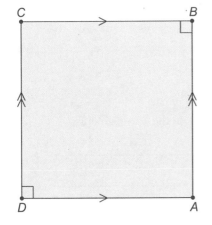

> $|CD| // |BA|$
>
> $|CB| \perp |KD|$ $|DA| // |CB|$
>
> $|CD| \perp |DA|$ $|DA| // |AB|$
>
> $|AB| \perp |CB|$

Activity 11.12

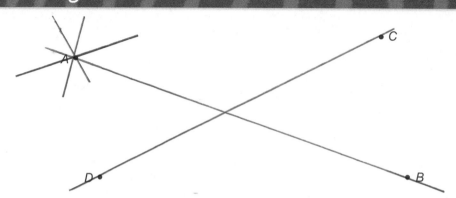

(i) Draw three lines through the point A.

(ii) How many lines could be drawn through the point A? __360__

(iii) Draw a line through the points A and B. What is this line called? __AB__

(iv) Can you draw any other line that goes through the points A and B? __No__

(v) Draw a line through the points C and D. What is this line called? __CD__

(vi) Can you draw any other line that goes through the points C and D? __No__

(vii) The point where the two lines meet is called the point of __intersection__ of the two lines.

Activity 11.13

(i) Draw a line segment [PQ] that is 10 cm in length.

P   10cm   X   Q

(ii) Mark a point X anywhere on the line segment between P and Q. Measure each of the line segments:

$|PQ|$ = __10cm__ $|PX|$ = __6.5 cm__ $|XQ|$ = __3.5cm__

(iii) Calculate $|PX| + |XQ|$ __6.5 + 3.5 = 10cm__

(iv) Is $|PQ| = |PX| + |XQ|$? __Yes__

What does this show? __$|PX| + |XQ| = |PQ|$ putting another__
__point does not effect length.__

Activity 11.14

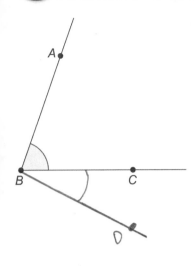

(i) What type of angle is ∠ABC? _acute_

(ii) Using your protractor, find |∠ABC|. _70°_ .

(iii) On the diagram, draw ∠DBC such that |∠DBC| = 30°.

(iv) Without using a protractor, find |∠ABD| = _100°_

(v) Check your answer using a protractor.

Activity 11.15

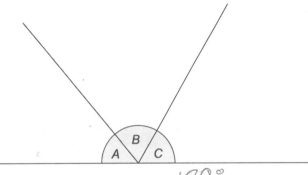

(i) Without using a protractor, find |∠A| + |∠B| + |∠C| = _180°_

Give a reason for your answer. _Straight Angle_

(ii) If |∠A| = 50° and |∠B| = 70°, find the measure of angle ∠C:

|∠C| = _60°_

Show how you got your answer.

50 + 70 = 120
180 - 120 = 60°

(iii) Check your answer using a protractor.

Activity 11.16

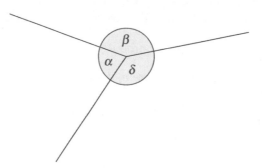

(i) Without using a protractor, find $|\angle\alpha| + |\angle\beta| + |\angle\delta| =$ __360°__

Give a reason for your answer. __full rotation__

_____

(ii) Using a protractor, find:

$|\angle\alpha| =$ __75°__ $|\angle\beta| =$ __150°__

(iii) Without using a protractor, find:

$|\angle\delta| =$ __45°__

Activity 11.17

(i) Draw a line parallel to the line *l* through the point *P*.

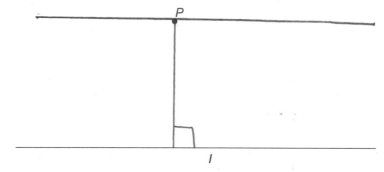

(ii) Put a symbol on each line to show that they are parallel. __||__

(iii) Is it possible to draw another line through *P* that is parallel to the line *l*?

__No__

(iv) Is it possible to draw a line through *P* that is perpendicular to the line *l*? __Yes__
If yes, draw it on the above diagram.

Constructions I chapter 12

 Activity 12.1

- Place the compass point on point *O*.
- Draw a circle of radius 6 cm.
- Where the circle intersects the lines, mark as points *A, B, C, D, E, F, G* and *H*, moving in a clockwise direction.
- Draw lines from *A* to *C, C* to *E, E* to *G*, and *G* to *A*.

(i) What type of shape is this? _____

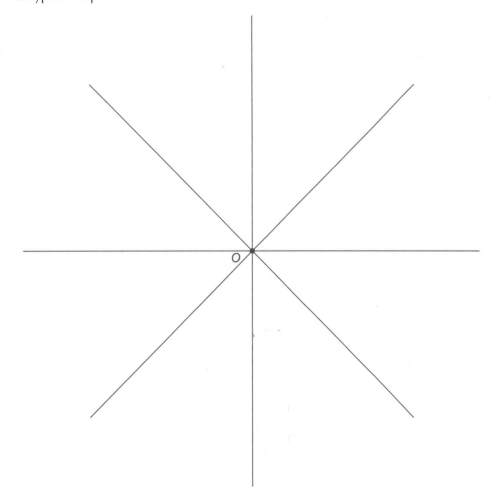

- Now draw the line segments [*AB*], [*BC*], [*CD*], [*DE*], [*EF*], [*FG*], [*GH*] and [*HA*].

(ii) Can you identify this new shape? _____

Activity 12.2

1. On the protractor, draw the following angles:

   (i) $|\angle 1| = 45°$

   (ii) $|\angle 2| = 75°$

   (iii) $|\angle 3| = 90°$

   (iv) $|\angle 4| = 130°$

   (v) $|\angle 5| = 165°$

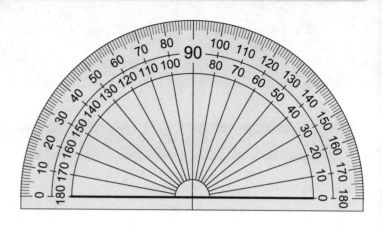

 Activity 12.3

Construct the bisector of $\angle ABC$. Check your construction using a protractor.

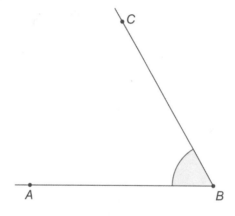

 Activity 12.4

Construct the bisector of $\angle DEF$.

- You might have to make sure that your overlapping arcs intersect properly.
- Do this by increasing the compass width for the second pair of arcs.
- Check your construction using a protractor.

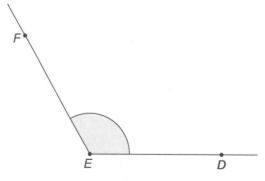

Construct the perpendicular bisector of the line segment [AB].
Check your construction using a protractor and ruler.

A ●————————————————————————————————● B

Construct a line perpendicular to the line *l*, passing through the point *A* on the line *l*.
Check your construction using a protractor.

l

A

Using a set square or protractor, construct a line perpendicular to the line *p*, passing through the point *D* on the line *p*.

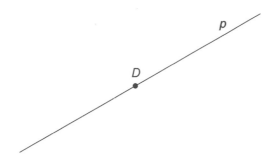

p

D

CONSTRUCTIONS I

12

Using **a compass and a straight edge**, construct a line parallel to the line *m*, passing through the point *A*.

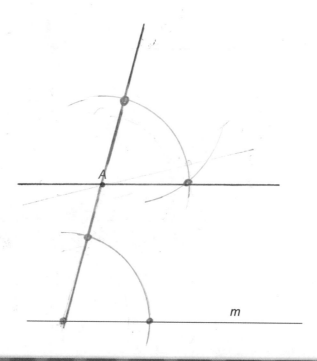

Activity 12.9

Using a **set square**, construct a line parallel to the line *b*, passing through the point *F*.

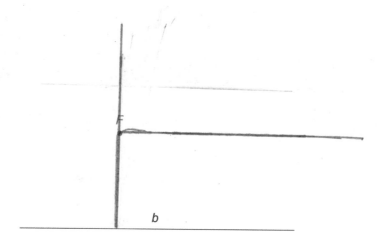

Activity 12.10

- Line up your set square with the line segment [BE].
- Place a ruler directly underneath the set square.
- Slide the set square along the ruler until you reach point D.
- Using the set square, draw a line segment from the point D to the line segment [AB].
- Slide the set square along the ruler until you reach point C.
- Using the set square, draw a line segment from the point C to the line segment [AB].
- Label the points of intersection with [AB].
- Use your ruler to check if [AB] has been divided into three equal parts.

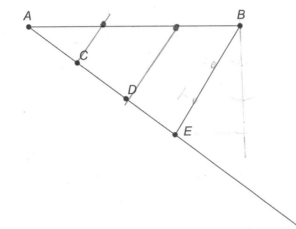

Activity 12.11

Divide the line segment [AB] into **three** equal parts. Check your construction using a compass or ruler.

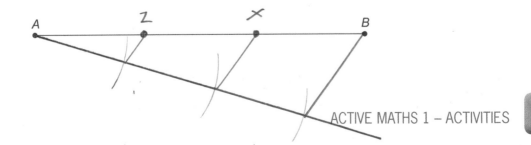

Activity 12.12

Construct a line segment 6 cm in length on the given ray.

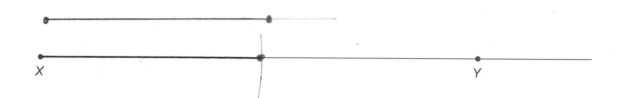

X   Y

Activity 12.13

Construct a line segment of length 7 cm on the given ray.

T   S

Activity 12.14

Using a protractor, construct the following angles using the ray AB].

  (i) $|\angle ABC| = 30°$

 (ii) $|\angle ABD| = 90°$

(iii) $|\angle ABE| = 120°$

(iv) $|\angle ABF| = 260°$

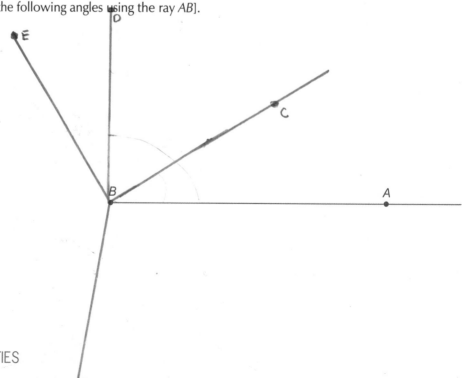

Activity 13.1

In the following diagram, name and colour in the angle that is vertically opposite to angle *A* in each case.

(i)

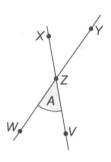

Name: _____

(ii)

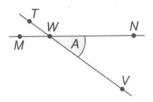

Name: _____

(iii)

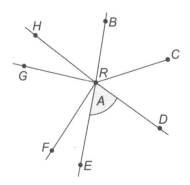

Name: _____

(iv)

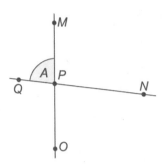

Name: _____

(v)

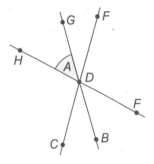

Name: _____

(vi)

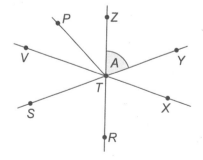

Name: _____

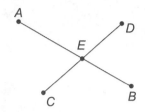

Activity 13.2

(i) Look at the diagram below. Measure the following angles using a protractor.

$|\angle AED| =$

$|\angle DEB| =$

$|\angle BEC| =$

$|\angle CEA| =$

(ii) Are any angles equal in measurement? _____

If yes, which angles are equal to each other?

(iii) Now consider the angles in the diagram below. Without using a protractor, which angles (if any) are equal to each other?

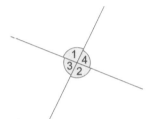

Activity 13.3

(i) In the space provided, draw two lines that intersect each other.

(ii) Mark the point of intersection of the two lines.

(iii) Label the angles at this point of intersection as $\angle 1, \angle 2, \angle 3, \angle 4$.

(iv) Measure all four angles at the point of intersection:

$|\angle 1| =$ _____ $|\angle 2| =$ _____

$|\angle 3| =$ _____ $|\angle 4| =$ _____

(v) Which angles are equal to each other? _____

(vi) What letter of the alphabet does your drawing look like? _____

(vii) In the box provided, write down a rule (theorem) that sums up what you have learned
so far in this activity:

Theorem:

 Activity 13.4

In the following diagram, colour in the angle that is alternate to angle *A* in each case.

(i)

(ii)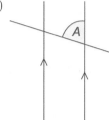

(iii)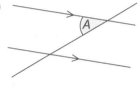

(iv)

 Activity 13.5

(i) Look at the diagram below. Measure all the angles
that are numbered.

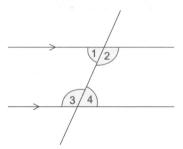

(ii) List the angles that are equal to each other.

Angles	Measure

(iii) What are these angles called?

_____

 Activity 13.6

(i) In the diagram below, draw a line that cuts across the two given lines.

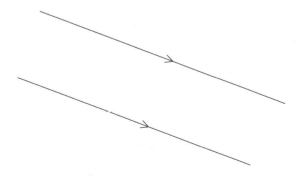

(ii) What is the name for the line you have just drawn? _____

(iii) What do the arrows mean on the other two lines? _____

(iv) Now find **two pairs** of alternate angles and colour them in on the diagram.

(v) Measure each pair of alternate angles using a protractor:

$|\angle 1| = $ _____ $|\angle 2| = $ _____

$|\angle 3| = $ _____ $|\angle 4| = $ _____

(vi) Trace the letter of the alphabet on the diagram that helps you identify alternate angles. What letter is this?

_____

(vii) In the box provided, write down a rule (theorem) that states what you have learned so far in this activity:

Theorem:

Activity 13.7

Examine the lines shown on the right.

(i) Do you think the lines are parallel?

_____

(ii) Draw a transversal (a line that crosses the two lines). _____

(iii) Mark and measure a pair of alternate angles.

(iv) Are the alternate angles equal in measure? _____

(v) Using the answer from part (iv), what conclusion can be drawn about the two given lines?

_____

_____

_____

Activity 13.8

In the following diagram, colour in the corresponding angle to angle A in each case.

(i)

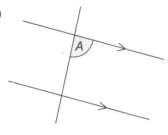

(iii)

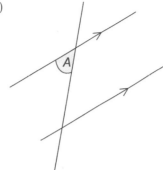

(ii)

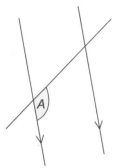

(iv)

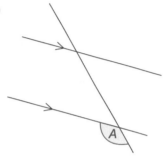

Activity 13.9

(i) Look at the diagram below.

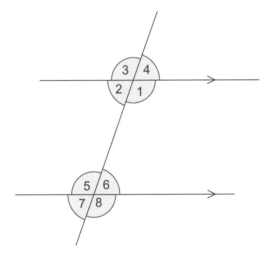

List four pairs of corresponding angles.

Pair 1	
Pair 2	
Pair 3	
Pair 4	

(ii) Measure all eight angles using a protractor.

$|\angle 1| =$	$|\angle 5| =$
$|\angle 2| =$	$|\angle 6| =$
$|\angle 3| =$	$|\angle 7| =$
$|\angle 4| =$	$|\angle 8| =$

(iii) Are the angles for each pair in part (i) equal in measure?

_____

Activity 13.10

(i) In the diagram below, draw a line that cuts across the two lines shown.

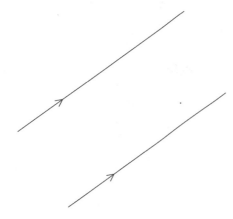

(ii) Now pick two pairs of corresponding angles, number the angles 1, 2, 3 and 4 and colour them in on the diagram.

(iii) Measure each pair of corresponding angles, using a protractor.

$|\angle 1| = $ _____ $|\angle 2| = $ _____

$|\angle 3| = $ _____ $|\angle 4| = $ _____

(iv) Trace the letter of the alphabet on the diagram that helps you identify corresponding angles. What letter is this? _____

(v) In the box provided, write down a theorem that shows what you have learned so far in this activity.

Theorem:

Activity 13.11

Consider the lines in the diagram below.

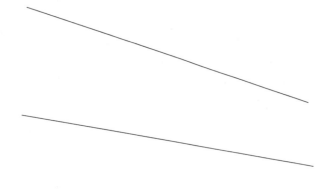

(i) Are the lines parallel? _____

(ii) Draw a transversal.

(iii) Justify your answer to part (i) by measuring a pair of corresponding angles and commenting on the result.

(i) Label this shape.

_____

(ii) Measure the distance from:

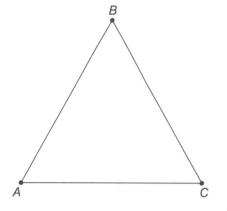

> A to B = _____
>
> B to C = _____
>
> C to B = _____

What do you notice? _____

(iii) Using a protractor, find $|\angle A|$ and write down the answer: _____

(iv) Find $|\angle B|$ and $|\angle C|$:

> $|\angle B|$ = _____
>
> $|\angle C|$ = _____

What do you notice? _____

(v) What name is given to this type of triangle? _____

(vi) Calculate $|\angle A| + |\angle B| + |\angle C|$ = _____

(i) Label this shape.

_____

(ii) Measure the following distances:

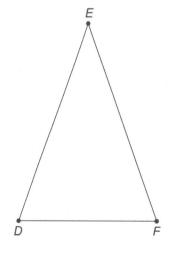

> $|DE|$ = _____
>
> $|EF|$ = _____
>
> $|DF|$ = _____

What do you notice? _____

(iii) Measure the following angles:

$|\angle D| =$ _____ $|\angle E| =$ _____ $|\angle F| =$ _____

What do you notice? _____

(iv) What name is given to this type of triangle? _____

(v) Calculate $|\angle D| + |\angle E| + |\angle F| =$ _____

 **Activity 13.14**

(i) Label this shape.

_____

(ii) Measure the following distances:

$|XY| =$ _____

$|YZ| =$ _____

$|XZ| =$ _____

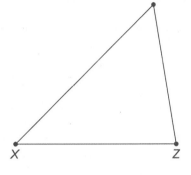

(iii) What do you notice? _____

(iv) Measure the following angles:

$|\angle X| =$ _____ $|\angle Y| =$ _____ $|\angle Z| =$ _____

(v) What do you notice? _____

(vi) What name is given to this type of triangle? _____

(vii) Calculate $|\angle X| + |\angle Y| + |\angle Z| =$ _____

(viii) From your investigations, the angles in a triangle add up to: _____

Activity 13.15

(i) Measure the following angles:

$|\angle A| =$ _____

$|\angle B| =$ _____

$|\angle C| =$ _____

(ii) Find:

$|\angle A| + |\angle B| + |\angle C| =$ _____

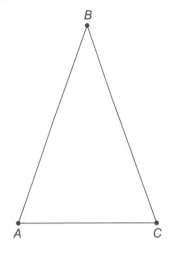

(iii) The length of the side [AB] =

(iv) The length of the side [BC] =

(v) The length of the side [AC] =

(vi) Which sides are equal? _____

(vii) Which angles are equal? _____

(viii) What do you notice about the equal sides and angles? _____

(ix) In the box provided, write down a theorem that describes what you have learned in this activity:

Theorem:

Activity 13.16

(i) Measure the following angles:

$|\angle X| =$ _____

$|\angle Y| =$ _____

$|\angle Z| =$ _____

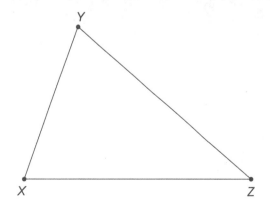

(ii) Calculate:

$$|\angle X| + |\angle Y| + |\angle Z| =$$

(iii) Mark on the triangle the sides that you think will be equal in length.

(iv) Now check your answer by measuring the length of each side:

$$|XY| = \qquad\qquad |YZ| = \qquad\qquad |XZ| =$$

 Activity 13.17

(i) Draw out any triangle on a piece of paper. Mark the angles as shown in the diagram.

(ii) Now tear off each angle as shown.

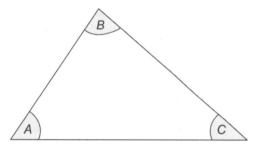

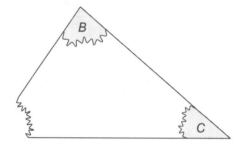

(iii) Now place the torn-out angles side by side. What type of angle does this make?

_____

(iv) How many degrees are there in this type of angle? _____

(v) In the box provided, write down a theorem that describes what you have learned about the sum of the angles in a triangle:

> **Theorem:**

(i) Measure the angles:

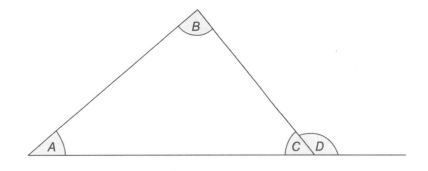

$|\angle A| =$ _____

$|\angle B| =$ _____

$|\angle C| =$ _____

$|\angle D| =$ _____

(ii) What name is given to $\angle D$? _____

(iii) What name is given to $\angle A$ and $\angle B$? _____

(iv) Find $|\angle A| + |\angle B| =$ _____

What do you notice? _____

(v) Write down a theorem that this activity shows:

Theorem:

Activity 13.19

(i) Which two angles when added together will equal angle G in measure?

_____

Why? _____

_____

(ii) Check your answer by measuring the angles:

$|\angle D| =$ _____

$|\angle E| =$ _____

$|\angle F| =$ _____

$|\angle G| =$ _____

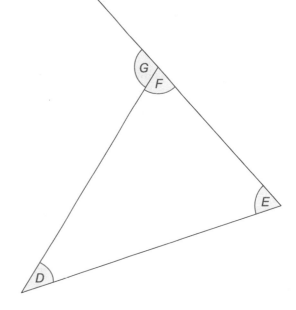

(iii) Complete: $|\angle | + |\angle | = |\angle |$

1. (i) Measure the following distances:

A to B = _____ B to C = _____

|CD| = _____ |DA| = _____

What do you notice? _____

(ii) Find |∠ABC|: _____

(iii) Measure the following angles:

|∠BCD| = _____ |∠CDA| = _____ |∠DAB| = _____

What do you notice? _____

2. (i) Draw a line from B to D. What do we call this line? _____

(ii) Draw a line from A to C. Where the two lines meet, mark this as point E.

Find |∠AED| = _____

(iii) Are there any other angles that are equal to |∠AED|?

(a) = _____ (b) = _____ (c) = _____

(iv) Measure the distance from A to E: _____

(v) List the other line segments that you think would be equal to |AE|:

(a) = _____ (b) = _____ (c) = _____

3. (i) List all the properties (things) you have learned about this shape:

(ii) What shape is this? _____

1. (i) Measure the following distances:

B _____ C

A _____ D

A to B = _____   B to C = _____

|CD| = _____ |DA| = _____

What do you notice? _____

(ii) Find |∠ABC|: _____

(iii) Measure the following angles:

|∠BCD| = _____ |∠CDA| = _____

|∠DAB| = _____

What do you notice? _____

2. (i) Draw a line from B to D and from A to C. Where these two lines intersect, mark this as point E.
Find:

|AE| = _____   and |EC| = _____

|BE| = _____   and |ED| = _____

What do you notice? _____

(ii) Measure the angles: |∠AED| = _____ and |∠AEB| = _____

Do you get the same result as for the square in the previous Activity? _____

3. (i) List all the properties (things) you have learned about this shape:

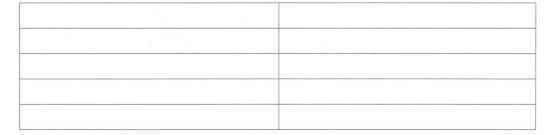

(ii) What shape is this? _____

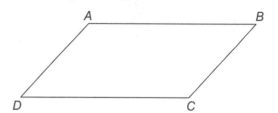

(i) Draw a line from *B* to *D* and a line from *A* to *C*.
Mark the point of intersection as *E*.

(ii) Investigate the properties of this shape and write
them down in the boxes below.
The first one is done for you:

Properties	What lengths of sides or angles (name and measure) did you use?
Opposites sides are equal in length	|AD| = |BC| = _____ cm |AB| = |DC| = _____ cm

(iii) What shape is this? _____

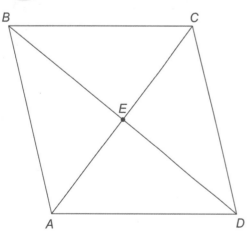

(i) What are its properties? Show the measurements:

Properties	What lengths of sides or angles (name and measure) did you use?

(ii) What shape is this? _____

GEOMETRY II: THEOREMS

13

Activity 13.24

1. (i) *ABCD* is a parallelogram. Find:

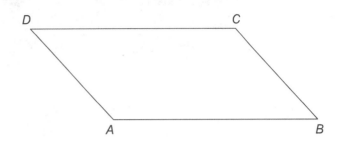

|AB| = _____

|BC| = _____

|CD| = _____

|DA| = _____

(ii) Opposite sides of a parallelogram are: _____

(iii) Find:

|∠DAB| = _____ |∠ABC| = _____

|∠BCD| = _____ |∠CDA| = _____

(iv) Opposite angles in a parallelogram are: _____

(v) Write down a theorem that describes these properties:

Theorem:

2. (i) Draw one line from *A* to *C* and another from *D* to *B*.

These lines are called: _____

(ii) Label the point where these lines meet as the point *X*. Find:

|AC| = _____ |AX| = _____ |XC| = _____

|BD| = _____ |BX| = _____ |XD| = _____

(iii) Write down a theorem that describes these properties:

Theorem:

Activity 14.1

1. The following text is taken from an article about the recycling of electronic waste. It shows how journalists use statistics to help us understand the news. Read the piece and answer the questions.

European Recycling Platform (ERP)

In 2008, the ERP collected 250 tonnes of electronic waste in Kerry – that's the equivalent in weight of 50,000 Sam Maguire Cups or 36 double-decker buses. In the first six months of 2009, the ERP collected 56 tonnes of electronic waste in Kerry – that's the equivalent in weight of 11,200 Sam Maguire Cups or eight double-decker buses.

(i) How many tonnes of electronic waste was collected in 2008?

250 tonnes of electronic waste

(ii) According to the article, what is the weight of 50,000 Sam Maguire cups?

The electronic waste.

(iii) Using the information in the piece, calculate the weight of a double-decker bus.
Give your answer to the nearest tonne.

(iv) In the first six months of 2009, the ERP collected 56 tonnes of electronic waste. If the waste was disposed of at the same rate for the next six months, predict the total amount that was recycled in 2009.

(v) If 50,000 Sam Maguire Cups weigh 250 tonnes, is the writer correct to say that 11,200 Sam Maguire Cups weigh 56 tonnes? Explain your answer.

Activity 14.2

This is an article on the number of pupils in Irish primary schools. It is based on a study carried out using data from the Central Statistics Office. Read the article and answer the questions that follow.

Surge in Pupil Numbers in Primary Schools

The number of births in Ireland last year rose to 72,620, compared to 48,255 fifteen years ago. This means that there will be over 500,000 primary school pupils for the next several years. Inward migration has also helped to push up the number of children enrolling in schools. In 2000, the number of primary school children was 440,000. In 2005, this number had risen to 457,889 and it has been rising since. This growth in numbers is expected to reach second level by 2016, with an increase of 51,500 secondary school pupils. As a result, it is estimated that 50 new schools will be needed at this level.

(i) According to the writer, how many new secondary schools do we need to build in the coming years?

_____

(ii) If this article was written in 2008, then in what year were there 48,255 births?

(iii) Between 2000 and 2005, the number of primary school children increased. Find this increase.

Activity 14.3

State whether the following data is **categorical** or **numerical**. If the data is numerical, say whether it is **discrete** or **continuous**. If the data is categorical, say whether it is **ordinal** or **nominal**.

(i) Shoe sizes of students in your class

Numerical — discrete

(ii) The heights of students in your class

Numerical - continuous

(iii) The colours of cars in the car park

(iv) The number of students in each classroom at 9.00 a.m.

(v) The eye colour of students in your class

(vi) The grades in a mathematics test

(vii) The favourite colours of students in your class

Activity 14.4

1. Give two examples of **categorical** data. (Do not use the examples in Activity 14.3.)

(i) _____

(ii) _____

2. Give two examples of **numerical** data. (Do not use the examples in Activity 14.3.)

(i) _____

(ii) _____

Activity 14.5

1. Using Excel, generate seven random numbers between 1 and 50. Write the numbers below.

2. Assign a number to each student in the class. Now use Excel to generate three random numbers. Write down the names of the three students who have been assigned these numbers.

3. Select any three numbers between 1 and 30. Write your numbers below.

4. Working in pairs and using Excel, generate five sets of three random numbers between 1 and 30.

5. Were any of the sets of three numbers in Q. 4 the same as your selection in Q. 3?

Activity 14.6

1. Complete the following questionnaire by ticking the relevant box or entering a number.

Q. 1 Are you

Male ☐   Female ✓

Q. 2 Are you a

First Year student ✓   Second Year student ☐   Third Year student ☐

Q. 3 What is your natural hair colour?

Dark brown ☐   Light brown ✓   Black ☐

Blonde ☐   Red ☐   Other ☐

Q. 4 Do you believe that you have too many exams at school?

Yes ☐   No ✓   Uncertain ☐

Q. 5 Which would you prefer to be?

Rich ☐   Famous ☐   Happy ☐   Healthy ✓

Q. 6 In a typical week how many text messages do you send?

1

Q. 7 How much phone credit do you use each week?

Q. 8 Approximately how many hours per week do you spend on homework?

2

2. Write down the type of data generated by each question in the questionnaire.

Q. 1 _____

Q. 2 _____

Q. 3 _____

Q. 4 _____

Q. 5 _____

Q. 6 _____

Q. 7 _____

Q. 8 _____

Angela, who studies woodwork, has decided to make and sell garden seats. However, she is not quite sure of the type of garden seat that would sell best in her neighbourhood. Design a questionnaire that Angela could use as part of a survey to find which type of garden seat she should make. Have at least seven questions in your questionnaire.

Q. 1 _____

_____

Q. 2 _____

_____

Q. 3 _____

_____

Q. 4 _____

_____

Q. 5 _____

_____

Q. 6 _____

_____

Q. 7 _____

_____

Activity 14.8

Use the following data to complete the frequency table below.

1	2	4	3	2	2
2	3	6	2	1	3
1	4	2	3	5	3
2	3	1	4	5	5
2	2	3	4	1	1

Number	1	2	3	4	5	6
Tally						
Frequency						

(i) How many numbers are on the list?

(iv) How many 4's are on the list?

(ii) Which number appears most often?

(v) What fraction of the list is made up of 3's?

(iii) Which number appears least often?

Activity 14.9

Survey your class to find out each student's family size (exclude parents). Then complete the frequency table below.

Size	1	2	3	4	5	6	7
Tally							
Number							

(i) How many students are in the class?

(ii) What is the most common family size in your class?

(iii) What is the least common family size?

STATISTICS

Activity 14.10

Complete the sentences from the list of words below.

Primary   **Discrete**   **Survey**
Continuous   **Secondary**   **Data**

(i) In statistics, an unordered list is called _____

(ii) A method of collecting data _____

(iii) We call data that is countable _____

(iv) Data that is not countable is _____

(v) Data collected by the person who uses it is _____

(vi) Data taken from the newspaper is _____

Activity 14.11

The following bar chart shows shoe sizes for a class.
Using the bar chart, complete the frequency table below.

Size	3	4	5	6	7	8	9	10
Number								

(i) What is the most common shoe size?

(ii) What sizes are the least common sizes?

(iii) How many students were present on the day the survey was carried out?

Activity 14.12

Conduct your own survey to find the distribution of shoe sizes in your class.
Complete the frequency table, and draw the bar chart.

Size							
Number							

(i) What is the most common shoe size?

(ii) What sizes are the least common sizes?

(iii) How many students were present on the day the survey was carried out?

STATISTICS

Activity 14.13

Using your protractor, measure the angle in each sector and complete the table below.

Pie chart

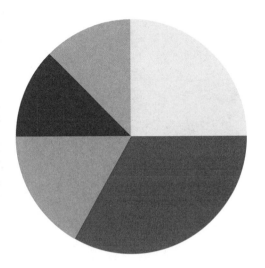

Colour	Angle
	90°

Activity 14.14

The following stem-and-leaf plot displays the marks of a group of students in a mathematics test.

Stem	Leaf
4	1, 2, 3, 5
5	2, 2, 4, 8, 9, 9
6	1, 4, 5, 5, 6, 8
7	1, 1, 2, 2, 3, 5, 7, 9
8	2, 3, 4, 6
9	5, 6, 7
10	0, 0 Key: 9|5 = 95

(i) How many students sat the test?

(ii) What is the best mark?

(iii) What is the lowest mark?

(iv) How many students got a mark of 72?

(v) What is the difference between the lowest mark and the highest mark?

STATISTICS

Activity 14.15

Put the following data on a stem-and-leaf plot.

60	52	81	73	95
97	86	84	68	83
68	86	73	85	59
73	47	73	96	56

Stem	Leaf
4	
5	
6	
7	
8	
9	Key:

Activity 14.16

Here are the heights in centimetres (correct to the nearest centimetre) of a sample of students, randomly selected from the CensusAtSchools website.

170	171	177	150	163	176	170
169	169	160	162	166	160	169
165	140	168	148	160	157	163
163	175	145	152	160	159	144

(i) How many students were surveyed?

(ii) Complete the following frequency distribution:

Height (cm)	135.5–145.5	145.5–155.5	155.5–165.5	165.5–175.5	175.5–185.5
Tally					
Frequency					

Note: 135.5–145.5 means greater than or equal to 135.5 but less than 145.5.

(iii) Using graph paper, represent the data on a histogram.
Put the height on the horizontal axis.

Six bags contain coins as in the diagram below. The value of each coin is given on top, and the number of coins in each bag is given underneath.

Bag 1(2c)   Bag 2(5c)   Bag 3(10c)   Bag 4(20c)   Bag 5(50c)   Bag 6(€2)

60   50   40   50   20   10

(i)   Using the graph paper below, draw a bar chart to represent the number of coins in each bag.

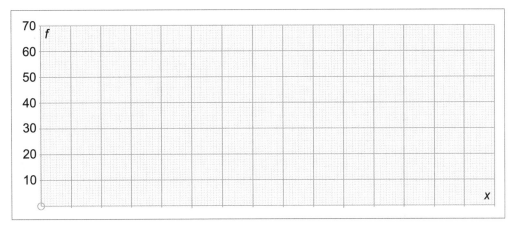

(ii) Calculate the mean number of coins per bag.

(iii) How many bags have less than the mean number of coins? _____

(iv) How many bags have more than the mean number of coins? _____

STATISTICS

(v) Calculate the total amount of money in the six bags.

(vi) Calculate the mean amount of money per bag (to the nearest cent).

(vii) How many bags have less than the mean amount of money? _____

(viii) How many bags have more than the mean amount of money? _____

(ix) Why do you think your answer to (viii) is smaller than your answer to (iv)?

_____

_____

Activity 14.18

The following are the marks received by 25 students in a maths test:

98, 85, 76, 83, 74, 85, 62, 79, 85, 89, 98, 87, 92, 84, 63, 28, 49, 88, 87, 92, 83, 79, 75, 68, 75

(i) Rank the data.

(ii) Find the range.

(iii) Do you think the range is a true reflection of the spread of this data? Explain.

_____

_____

_____

Activity 14.19

1. In a recent survey, Morning Delight Cereals asked young people to indicate their favourite breakfast cereal. The result of the survey was as follows: 35% preferred Morning Delight Krispies, 30% preferred Morning Delight Porridge and 15% indicated that they preferred other cereals. The survey was conducted on Grafton Street in Dublin. Morning Delight intend to use the results in an advertisement, claiming that Morning Delight cereals are the country's most popular cereals. List **three** aspects of the survey that you think are wrong or misleading.

(i) _____

_____

(ii) _____

_____

(iii) _____

_____

2. 'The best holiday destinations abroad offer more activities and a better holiday than most Irish resorts.' Is this a misleading statement? Explain.

_____

_____

_____

_____

_____

3. The following chart shows the points accumulated by the top three Premiership teams in the 2008–2009 season:

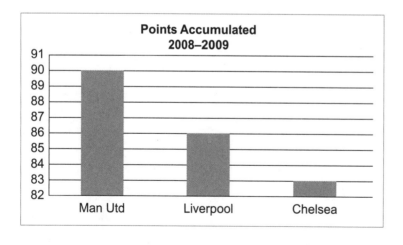

(i) What are your first impressions upon viewing the graph? What conclusions did you draw?

_____

_____

_____

(ii) How is this graph misleading?

_____

_____

4. 'Should people who work in the home be entitled to financial support from the state?' This question was put to listeners of a morning radio show. There was a large response to the survey, and 87% of listeners said that people who work at home should be entitled to state support. Give two reasons why this figure is misleading.

(i) _____

_____

(ii) _____

_____

5. After studying the heights of boys and girls who play basketball, a student comes to the conclusion that exercise from playing basketball makes people grow taller. Comment on the student's reasoning.

_____

_____

_____

_____

_____

STATISTICS

6. John believes he has found the cure for the common cold. His cure is one teaspoon of honey taken every morning for a period of two weeks. He randomly selects 10 students from all students in the school suffering from the cold. In two weeks, all 10 students had recovered. He concludes that he has made a major discovery. Comment on John's reasoning.

_____

_____

_____

_____

15 chapter

Indices and Reciprocals

1. (a) Write the following in index notation:

(i) $2 \times 2 \times 2$

(ii) $2 \times 2 \times 2 \times 2$

(iii) $2 \times 2 \times 2 \times 2 \times 2 \times 2 \times 2$

(b) $(2 \times 2 \times 2) \times (2 \times 2 \times 2 \times 2) = 2 \times 2 \times 2 \times 2 \times 2 \times 2 \times 2$.

Using your answers from part (a), evaluate $2^3 \times 2^4$ in index notation.

2. (a) Write the following in index notation:

(i) 3×3

(ii) $3 \times 3 \times 3$

(iii) $3 \times 3 \times 3 \times 3 \times 3$

(b) $(3 \times 3) \times (3 \times 3 \times 3) = 3 \times 3 \times 3 \times 3 \times 3$.

Using your answers from part (a), evaluate $3^2 \times 3^3$ in index notation.

3. (a) Write the following in index notation:

(i) $a \times a \times a$

(ii) $a \times a \times a \times a$

(iii) $a \times a \times a \times a \times a \times a \times a$

(b) $(a \times a \times a) \times (a \times a \times a \times a) = a \times a \times a \times a \times a \times a \times a$.

Using your answers from part (a), evaluate $a^3 \times a^4$ in index notation.

4. Using your results from above, write the following in index notation:

(i) $2^4 \times 2^5 =$ (ii) $5^4 \times 5^3 =$ (iii) $a^8 \times a^2 =$

5. Fill in the boxes:

(i) $4^3 \times 4^{\boxed{}} = 4^8$

(ii) $5^{\boxed{}} \times 5^2 = 5^{10}$

(iii) $2^{13} \times 2^4 = 2^{\boxed{}}$

(iv) $7^{\boxed{}} \times 7^6 = 7^8$

(v) $5^{\boxed{}} \times 5^3 = 5^{10}$

(vi) $2^{24} \times 2^4 = 2^{\boxed{}}$

6. Write $a^p \times a^q$ in simplest index form.

---

a^{pq} Activity 15.2

1. (a) Write the following in index notation:

(i) $5 \times 5 \times 5 \times 5$

(ii) 5×5

(iii) By dividing above and below by the common factors, write in index notation:

$$\frac{5 \times 5 \times 5 \times 5}{5 \times 5}$$

(b) Using your answers from (a), write $\dfrac{5^4}{5^2}$ in index notation:

2. (a) Write the following in index notation:

(i) $7 \times 7 \times 7 \times 7 \times 7 \times 7$

(ii) $7 \times 7 \times 7$

(iii) By dividing above and below by the common factors, write in index notation:

$$\frac{7 \times 7 \times 7 \times 7 \times 7 \times 7}{7 \times 7 \times 7}$$

(b) Using your answers from (a), write $\dfrac{7^6}{7^3}$ in index notation:

3. (a) Write the following in index notation:

(i) $a \times a \times a \times a \times a$

(ii) $a \times a$

(iii) $\dfrac{a \times a \times a \times a \times a}{a \times a}$

(b) Using your answers from part (a), write $\dfrac{a^5}{a^2}$ in index notation:

4. Fill in the boxes:

(i) $3^{12} \div 3^{\boxed{}} = 3^7$

(iii) $2^{12} \div 2^3 = 2^{\boxed{}}$

(v) $9^{\boxed{}} \div 9^3 = 9^{11}$

(ii) $6^{\boxed{}} \div 6^2 = 6^{10}$

(iv) $7^{\boxed{}} \div 7^6 = 7^8$

(vi) $8^{24} \div 8^4 = 8^{\boxed{}}$

5. Write $a^p \div a^q$ in simplest index form. $\boxed{}$

 Activity 15.3

1. Write in index notation:

$6 \times 6 \times 6$

$\boxed{}$

2. Write in index notation (ignore the brackets):

$(6 \times 6 \times 6) \times (6 \times 6 \times 6) \times (6 \times 6 \times 6) \times (6 \times 6 \times 6)$

$\boxed{}$

3. Using your result from Question 2, explain why $(6 \times 6 \times 6)^4 = 6^{12}$.

$\boxed{}$

4. Using your result from Question 3, explain why $(6^3)^4 = 6^{12}$.

$\boxed{}$

5. Write in index notation:

7×7

$\boxed{}$

6. Write in index notation (ignore the brackets):

$(7 \times 7) \times (7 \times 7) \times (7 \times 7) \times (7 \times 7) \times (7 \times 7)$

$\boxed{}$

7. Using your result from Question 6, explain why $(7 \times 7)^5 = 7^{10}$.

$\boxed{}$

8. Using your result from Question 7, explain why $(7^2)^5 = 7^{10}$.

$\boxed{}$

9. Write in index notation:

$a \times a$

[ ]

10. Write in index notation (ignore the brackets):

$(a \times a) \times (a \times a) \times (a \times a) \times (a \times a) \times (a \times a)$

[ ]

11. Using your result from Question 10, explain why $(a \times a)^5 = a^{10}$.

12. Using your result from Question 11, explain why $(a^2)^5 = a^{10}$.

13. Match each entry in column A with its index answer in column B. One has been done for you.

A
$9^3 \times 9^4$
$9^7 \div 9^2$
$(9^3)^5$
$9^7 \times 9^9$
$\dfrac{9^{16}}{9^8}$
9×9
$9^{20} \div 9^{19}$
$(9^5)^2$

B
9^8
9^5
9^{15}
9^7
9^{16}
9
9^{10}
9^2

1. Do the following multiplications:

(i) 5.2×10

(v) 5.2×10^5

(ii) 5.2×10^2

(vi) 5.2×10^6

(iii) 5.2×10^3

(vii) 5.2×10^7

(iv) 5.2×10^4

2. Using your results from Question 1, complete the following table:

$52 \div 10$	
$520 \div 10^2$	
$5,200 \div 10^3$	
$52,000 \div 10^4$	
$520,000 \div 10^5$	
$5,200,000 \div 10^6$	
$52,000,000 \div 10^7$	

What do you notice about all the answers?

3. Using the answers from Question 1, complete the following table.

1st Column	2nd Column
52	$5.2 \times 10^{\square}$
520	$5.2 \times 10^{\square}$
5,200	$5.2 \times 10^{\square}$
52,000	$5.2 \times 10^{\square}$
520,000	$5.2 \times 10^{\square}$
5,200,000	$5.2 \times 10^{\square}$
52,000,000	$5.2 \times 10^{\square}$

The numbers in the second column are the numbers from the first column written in scientific notation.

5.2×10^4

The number above is written in scientific notation. We call 5.2 the **coefficient**, 10 the **base** and 4 the **exponent**.

4. Complete the following table:

Number	Coefficient	Base	Exponent
6.8×10^5			
3.4×10^2	3.4	10	2
9.7×10^8			
1.15×10^{12}			
6.62×10^7			
4.19×10^4			
2.3×10			
6.0×10^{24}			

In scientific notation, the **coefficient** is always a number less than 10 (therefore, it cannot be 10) and greater than or equal to 1.

5. Which of the following numbers are written in scientific notation? Answer Yes (✓) or No (✗)

68×10^5	
3.4×10^2	
609×10^{24}	
6.621×10^7	
1.215×10^{12}	
419×10^4	
2.153×10	
97×10^8	

6. Write the following numbers in scientific notation:

(i) 35

(ii) 480

(iii) 570

(iv) 980

(v) 6,700

(vi) 340,000

(vii) 7,800,000

(viii) 770,000,000,000

16 chapter Applied Arithmetic

Activity 16.1

Calculate the gross tax for each of the following (the first has been done for you):

	Gross income	Tax rate	Gross tax
1	€25,000	20.00%	€25,000 × 0.2 = €5,000
2	€18,000	18.00%	
3	€34,000	22.00%	
4	€46,000	21.50%	
5	€78,000	23.00%	
6	€55,000	21.00%	
7	€60,000	20.00%	
8	€34,500	20.50%	
9	€17,500	21.50%	
10	€26,500	22.00%	

Calculate the tax payable for each of the following (the first has been done for you):

	Gross income	Tax rate	Gross tax	Tax credit	Tax payable
1	€25,000	20.00%	€25,000 × 0.2 = €5,000	€1,800	€5,000 – €1,800 = €3,200
2	€19,000	16.00%		€2,500	
3	€24,000	22.00%		€3,400	
4	€46,000	22.50%		€1,600	
5	€36,000	21.00%		€2,600	
6	€16,000	20.00%		€2,400	
7	€60,000	20.50%		€3,400	
8	€25,500	20.50%		€4,001	
9	€24,000	22.00%		€2,450	
10	€54,000	22.50%		€2,340	

Activity 16.3

Calculate the net income for each of the following (the first has been done for you):

			Gross tax	Tax payable	Net income
1	**Gross income**	€15,000	15,000 × 0.20 = €3,000	3,000 − 1,800 €1,200	15,000 − 1,200 €13,800
	Tax rate	20.00%			
	Tax credit	€1,800			
2	**Gross income**	€19,000			
	Tax rate	19.00%			
	Tax credit	€2,500			
3	**Gross income**	€24,000			
	Tax rate	21.50%			
	Tax credit	€3,400			
4	**Gross income**	€36,000			
	Tax rate	22.00%			
	Tax credit	€1,600			
5	**Gross income**	€39,000			
	Tax rate	18.00%			
	Tax credit	€2,600			
6	**Gross income**	€46,000			
	Tax rate	19.50%			
	Tax credit	€2,400			
7	**Gross income**	€78,000			
	Tax rate	21.00%			
	Tax credit	€3,400			
8	**Gross income**	€36,500			
	Tax rate	20.00%			
	Tax credit	€4,001			
9	**Gross income**	€41,500			
	Tax rate	22.00%			
	Tax credit	€2,450			
10	**Gross income**	€22,500			
	Tax rate	22.50%			
	Tax credit	€2,340			

Activity 16.4

Calculate the VAT on each of the following bills (the first has been done for you):

	Bill amount	VAT rate	VAT
1	€40,000.00	13.50%	€40,000 × 0.135 = €5,400
2	€400.00	12.50%	
3	€350.00	21.00%	
4	€86.00	21.50%	
5	€340.00	18.00%	
6	€2,500.00	19.50%	
7	€1,700.00	21.00%	
8	€3,500.50	20.00%	
9	€39.50	22.00%	
10	€3,330.00	22.50%	

Activity 16.5

The following bills are inclusive of VAT.

Find the total **before VAT** for each of the following (the first has been done for you):

	Total bill	VAT rate	Total before VAT
1	€567.50	13.50%	113.5% = €567.50 1% = $\frac{567.50}{113.5}$ = €5 100% = €5 × 100 = €500
2	€11,250.00	12.50%	
3	€42.35	21.00%	
4	€534.60	21.50%	
5	€4,295.20	18.00%	
6	€298.75	19.50%	
7	€786.50	21.00%	
8	€270.00	20.00%	
9	€4,209.61	22.00%	
10	€901.60	22.50%	

1. In the gas bill shown below, calculate the missing figures correct to one decimal place where necessary:

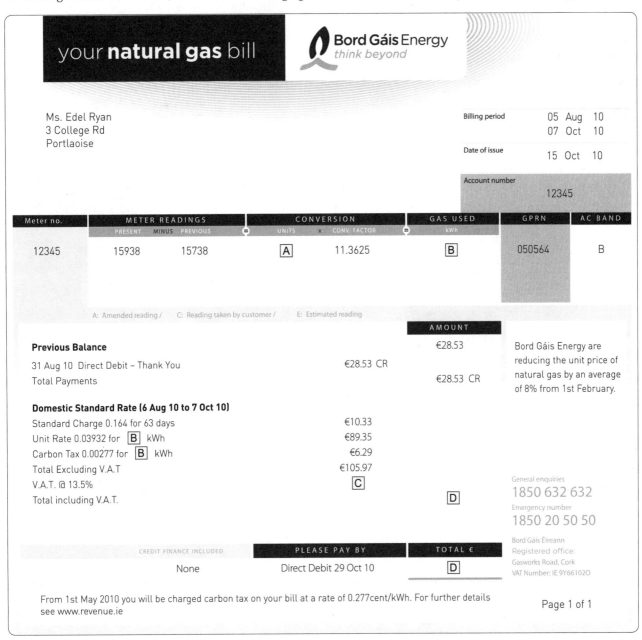

your natural gas bill

Bord Gáis Energy
think beyond

Ms. Edel Ryan
3 College Rd
Portlaoise

Billing period	05 Aug 10
	07 Oct 10
Date of issue	15 Oct 10

Account number
12345

Meter no.	METER READINGS			CONVERSION			GAS USED	GPRN	AC BAND
	PRESENT	MINUS PREVIOUS	=	UNITS	x CONV. FACTOR	=	kWh		
12345	15938	15738		A	11.3625		B	050564	B

A: Amended reading /   C: Reading taken by customer /   E: Estimated reading

	AMOUNT	
Previous Balance		€28.53
31 Aug 10 Direct Debit – Thank You	€28.53 CR	
Total Payments		€28.53 CR
Domestic Standard Rate (6 Aug 10 to 7 Oct 10)		
Standard Charge 0.164 for 63 days		€10.33
Unit Rate 0.03932 for [B] kWh		€89.35
Carbon Tax 0.00277 for [B] kWh		€6.29
Total Excluding V.A.T		€105.97
V.A.T. @ 13.5%		C
Total including V.A.T.		D

Bord Gáis Energy are reducing the unit price of natural gas by an average of 8% from 1st February.

General enquiries
1850 632 632
Emergency number
1850 20 50 50

Bord Gáis Éireann
Registered office:
Gasworks Road, Cork
VAT Number: IE 9Y66102O

| CREDIT FINANCE INCLUDED | PLEASE PAY BY | TOTAL € |
| None | Direct Debit 29 Oct 10 | D |

From 1st May 2010 you will be charged carbon tax on your bill at a rate of 0.277cent/kWh. For further details see www.revenue.ie

Page 1 of 1

[A] Number of units used this month	[C] VAT charged on this bill
[B] Gas used in kWh	[D] Total including VAT

2. In the telephone bill below, calculate the rate of VAT charged to the nearest percent:

meteor™

Meteor Mobile Communications Ltd, 4030 Kingswood Avenue, Citywest Business Park, Naas Road, Dublin 24

Bill Pay

Mr. ABC
123 A Street
Carlow

Account Name	Mr. ABC
Account Number	123456
Invoice Number	F6548
Date of Invoice	25/07/2008
Call Charges	25 June–24 July 2008
Min Commitment	25 July–24 August 2008

Previous Balance (incl. VAT)	Payments Received	Overdue Amount	Total Charges this Month (incl. VAT)	Total Amount Due (incl. VAT)
€ 61.66	€ 61.66	€ 0.00	€ 68.42	€ 68.42

SUMMARY OF MONTHLY CHARGES
Total payments this period – Thank you   61.36 CR

Overdue Amount (Due Immediately)   0.00

Current Monthly Charges (excl. VAT)   56.55
VAT   11.87

Total Current Amount   68.42

Current Amount Due by 11 August 2008   €68.42

Please Note: Non-payment may result in withdrawal of service without prior notice

Payment Method: Direct Debit. Your account will be debited on or after 11 August 2008

Workings

3. Calculate the missing figures on the telephone bill below:

meteor™

Meteor Mobile Communications Ltd, 4030 Kingswood Avenue, Citywest Business Park, Naas Road, Dublin 24

Bill Pay

Mr. ABC
123 A Street
Carlow

Account Name	Mr. ABC
Account Number	123456
Invoice Number	F6548
Date of Invoice	25/07/2008
Call Charges	25 June–24 July 2008
Min Commitment	25 July–24 August 2008

Previous Balance (incl. VAT)	Payments Received	Overdue Amount	Total Charges this Month (incl. VAT)	Total Amount Due (incl. VAT)
€ 61.66	€ 61.66	€ 0.00	€	€

National Calls 200 minutes @ 13c/min — (i)

International Calls 11 minutes @ €1.25/min — (ii)

Text messages 145 @ 5c — (iii)

Standing Charge — 40.00

Total Charges (exc VAT) — (iv)

VAT @ 21% (to nearest cent) — (v)

Total Charge this month — (vi)

Please Note: Non-payment may result in withdrawal of service without prior notice

Payment Method: Direct Debit. Your account will be debited on or after 11 August 2008

Workings

€ Activity 16.7

Calculate the percentage profit or loss for each of the following:

	Cost price	Selling price	Profit/loss	% Mark-up
1	€25.00		€5.00	
2	€30.00	€36.00		
3	€25.00	€15.00		
4		€24.00	−€12.00	
5	€5.00		€11.00	
6	€120.00		€66.00	
7	€1.50	€3.60		
8		€2.80	€2.10	
9	€130.00	€143.00		
10	€150.00	€120.00		

Calculate the final value and interest for each of the following loans/investments.

The first question has been done for you.

FORMULA

$F = P(1 + i)^t$

1	€50,000 was invested at 5% for 2 years at compound interest.

Final value:	Interest:
$F = 50,000 (1 + 0.05)^2$	Interest = $F - P$
$= 50,000 (1.05)^2$	$= 55,125 - 50,000$
$= 50,000 (1.1025)$	Interest = €5,125
$F = €55,125$	

2	€24,500 was invested at 3% for 1 year at compound interest.

Final value:	Interest:

3	€44,000 was invested at 3% for 2 years at compound interest.

Final value:	Interest:

4	€1,400 was borrowed at 10% for 3 years at compound interest.

Final value:	Interest:

5	€10,200,000 was borrowed at 3% for 3 years at compound interest.

Final value:	Interest:

6	€15,000 was borrowed at 3% for 1 year at compound interest.	
	Final value:	Interest:

7	€14,500 was invested at 4% for 2 years at compound interest.	
	Final value:	Interest:

8	€600 was borrowed at 5% for 2 years at compound interest.	
	Final value:	Interest:

9	€115,000 was invested at 21% for 2 years at compound interest.	
	Final value:	Interest:

10	€600 was borrowed at 2% for 1 year at compound interest.	
	Final value:	Interest:

 Activity 17.1

The following table shows the start time (24 hours) of various films in a cinema.

For each film:

(i) Show the start time on the clock face.

(ii) Calculate the finish time and draw this time on the clock face provided.

	Marmaduke	Despicable Me	Cats & Dogs	Diary of a Wimpy Kid
Start time	12:20	15:30	11:20	10:30
Running time	88 mins	95 mins	82 mins	93 mins
Finish time				

	Life As We Know It	Wall Street	Red	Ramona & Beezus
Start time	17:20	18:10	21:15	16:10
Running time	114 mins	133 mins	110 mins	103 mins
Finish time				

(iii) State one disadvantage of showing the time using a 12-hour clock face.

The following is part of the northbound Dart timetable for Sydney Parade.

06.10	06.40	06.55	07.08	07.25
07.40	07.53	08.10	08.17	08.25
08.40	08.47	08.55	09.08	09.17
09.25	09.40	09.55	10.10	10.25
10.38	10.55	11.10	11.23	11.25

(i) The next northbound train is due 15 minutes after the last time shown. What time is this train due?

_____

(ii) If this train is 3 minutes early, at what time does the train arrive? _____

(iii) A commuter arrives 1 minute after the 09.55 train. How long will they have to wait for the next train?

_____

(iv) Between 08.10 and 09.17, what is the longest time between trains? _____

(v) Between 10.10 and 11.23, what is the shortest time between trains? _____

(vi) A train arrives at the station at 12.10. The next two trains arrive at the station at intervals of 8 minutes. The next four trains should arrive at intervals of 9 minutes. However, the last train arrives 12 minutes after the previous one.

Show these times on the timetable below:

12.10	_____	_____	_____
_____	_____	_____	_____

The following are results of an athletics track competition in a school.

(i) Event: 100 m sprint

	1st	2nd	3rd
Time	16 secs	18.5 sec	20 sec

Fill in the following DST triangles and, hence, find the speed in metres per second of each student:

1st

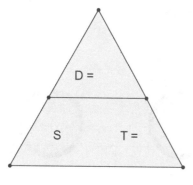

Speed _____

2nd

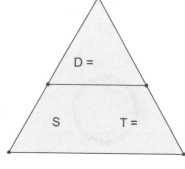

Speed _____

3rd

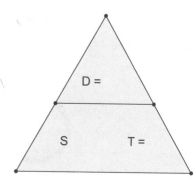

Speed _____

(ii) A number of students' speeds and times are calculated.

	Student A	Student B	Student C
Speed	5 m/s	15 km/h	5 m/s
Time	160 secs	40 mins	16 mins 40 secs

Fill in the following DST triangles and, hence, find the distance each student ran.

Student A

Student B

Student C

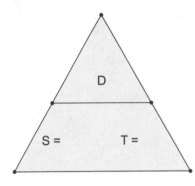

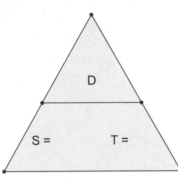

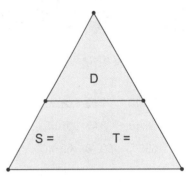

Distance _____

Distance _____

Distance _____

(iii) Usain Bolt's average speed for his world record was approximately 10.45 m/s.

(a) Using this speed, fill in the following DST triangles and, hence, find the time taken (to the nearest second).

200 m

1,000 m

42.195 km

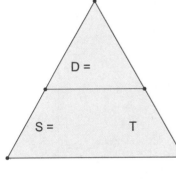

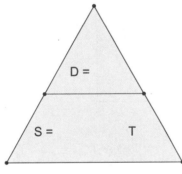

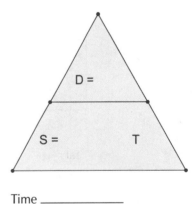

Time _____

Time _____

Time _____

(b) Change the time calculated to run 42.195 kilometres into hours, minutes and seconds: _____

(c) 42.195 kilometres is the distance run in a marathon. Explain why the time calculated to run this distance and the other times calculated may not be realistic.

_____

_____

_____

Area and Volume

Activity 18.1

1. By counting the 1 cm² squares, find the area and perimeter of each of the following shapes:

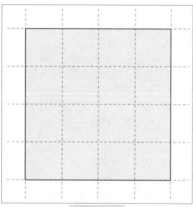

Figure 1

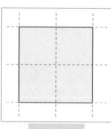

Figure 3

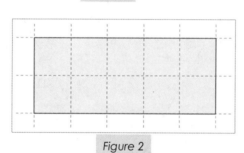

Figure 2

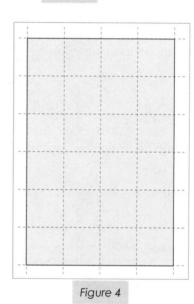

Figure 4

Fill in the table below:

Area	Length (*l*)	Width (*w*)	*l* × *w* =	Perimeter	2*l*	2*w*	2*l* + 2*w* =
Figure 1							
Figure 2							
Figure 3							
Figure 4							

What do you notice? _____

2. By counting the 1 cm² squares, find the area of the rectangle and of the blue shaded triangle.

> ■ Count a square that is more than half full as 1 cm².
> ■ Count a $\frac{1}{2}$ square as $\frac{1}{2}$ cm².
> ■ Count less than a $\frac{1}{2}$ square as zero.

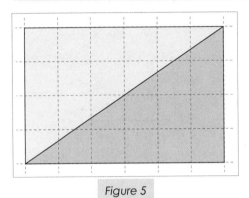

Figure 5

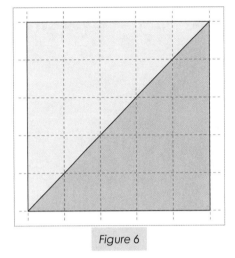

Figure 6

Fill in the table below:

	Area of triangle	Area of rectangle
Figure 5		
Figure 6		

What do you notice? _____

Write the formula for finding the area of a triangle. _____

A rectangle is made up of two triangles of _____ area.

3. Find the area of each shaded triangle in the following parallelograms.

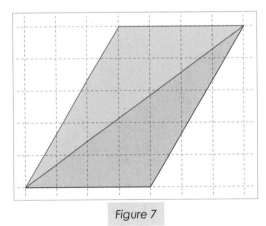

Figure 7

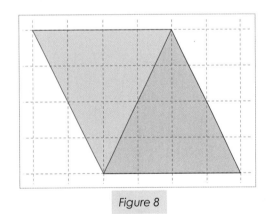

Figure 8

Fill in the table below:

	Area of blue triangle	Area of red triangle	Total area of shape
Figure 7			
Figure 8			

What do you notice? _____

Write the formula for finding the area of parallelogram: _____

Activity 18.2

You will need a piece of thread and a ruler to measure the length of the circumference of each circle.

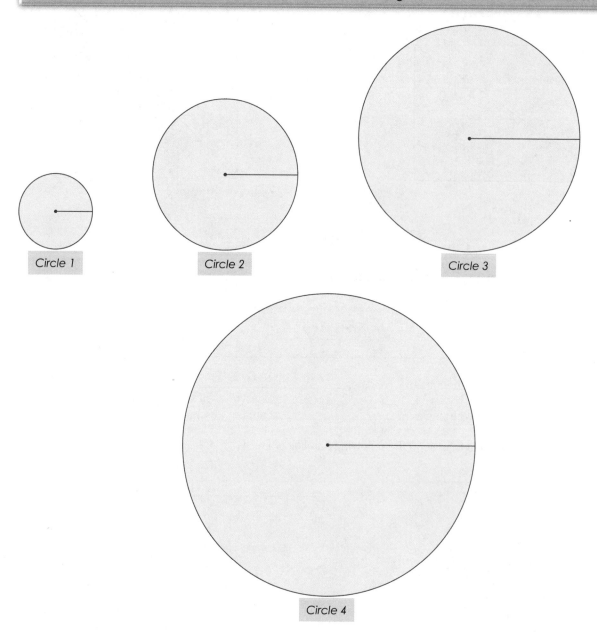

Circle 1

Circle 2

Circle 3

Circle 4

Fill in the table below:

	Circumference	Diameter	Circumference ÷ Diameter (1 decimal place)
Circle 1			
Circle 2			
Circle 3			
Circle 4			

What do you notice? _____

AREA AND VOLUME

By counting the number of 1 cm³ cubes, find the volume of each of the following shapes.

⬜ = 1 cm³

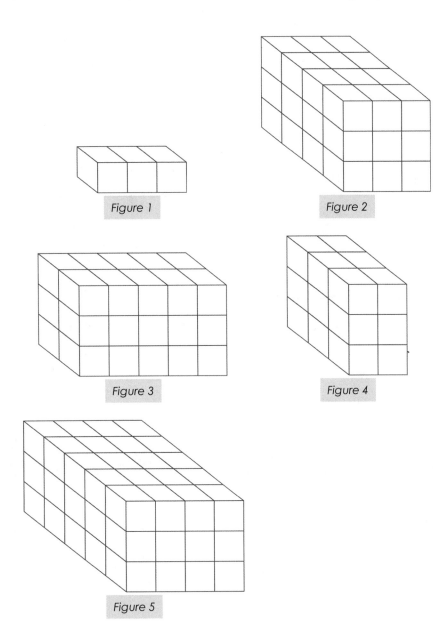

Figure 1

Figure 2

Figure 3

Figure 4

Figure 5

Fill in the table below:

Volume	Length (*l*)	Breadth (*b*)	Height (*h*)	*l* × *b* × *h* =
Figure 1				
Figure 2				
Figure 3				
Figure 4				
Figure 5				

Activity 18.4

1. Consider the nets of the following rectangular solids:

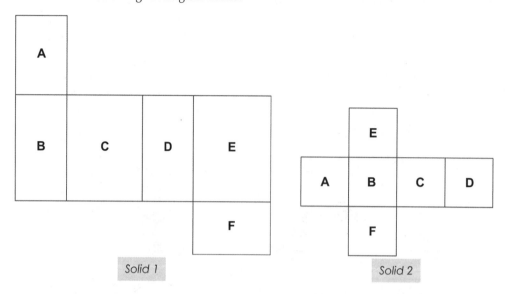

Solid 1

Solid 2

Find the area of each of the faces and fill in the table below.

	A	B	C	D	E	F	Total area
Solid 1							
Solid 2							

What is the other name given to the total area? _____

Activity 18.5

Measure the radius and height of each of the following cylinders:

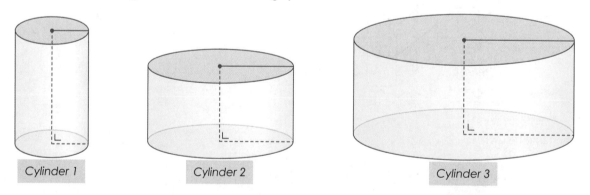

Cylinder 1   Cylinder 2   Cylinder 3

	Radius	Height	Area of circle πr^2 (Let $\pi = 3.14$)	Area of circle × height
Cylinder 1				
Cylinder 2				
Cylinder 3				

Area of circle × height gives us the _____ of the cylinder.

∴ Formula for volume of a cylinder = ⬚

1. Using the scaled diagram, estimate the height and length of each of the dinosaurs. The man is 1.75 m tall.

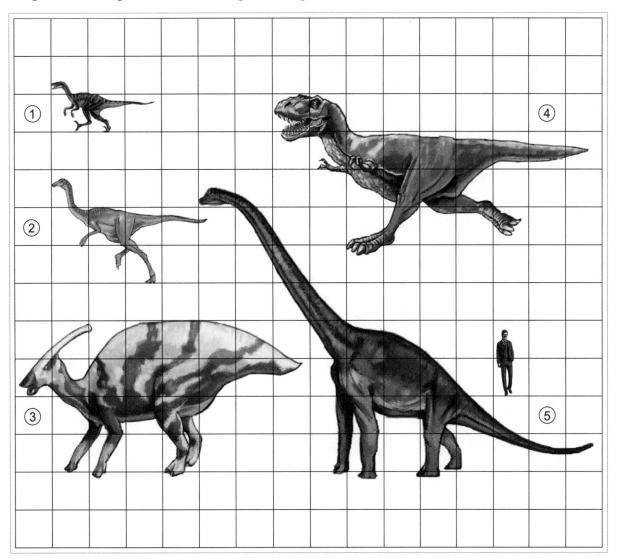

	Dinosaur 1	Dinosaur 2	Dinosaur 3	Dinosaur 4	Dinosaur 5
Height					
Length					

2. A scaled diagram for an office is shown. The wall *AB* is 8 m long.

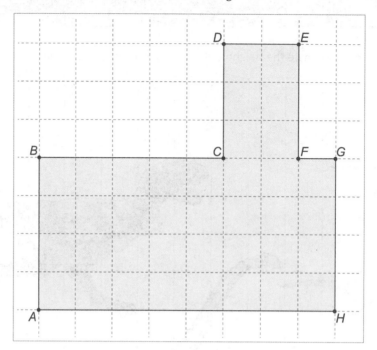

Fill in the following table.

Wall	Length (cm)	Actual length (m)
AB	4	8
BC		
CD		
DE		
EF		
FG		
GH		
HA		

The total area of the office is _____ m².

The scale for this diagram is ____ cm = ____ m.

This is written as ____ : ____.

Algebra: Solving Simultaneous Equations

x^2 Activity 19.1

Which of the following are the correct solutions for these simultaneous equations?

(i) $2x + y = 8$

$x + y = 6$

		$2x + y = 8$	$x + y = 6$	Correct solution
$x = 0$	$y = 5$	$2(0) + 5 \neq 8$	$0 + 5 \neq 6$	No
$x = 1$	$y = 0$			
$x = 1$	$y = 5$			
$x = 2$	$y = 4$			
$x = 4$	$y = 0$			

(ii) $2x + y = 12$

$2x - 2y = 6$

		$2x + y = 12$	$2x - 2y = 6$	Correct solution
$x = 0$	$y = 5$	$2(0) + (5) \neq 12$	$2(0) - 2(5) \neq 6$	No
$x = 1$	$y = 0$			
$x = 2$	$y = 5$			
$x = 3$	$y = 4$			
$x = 5$	$y = 2$			

x^2 **Activity 19.2**

1. (i) Complete the following table and, using these points, draw a line on the graph below (some have been done for you):

	2x + y = 8			Point
x = 0	2(0) + y = 8	0 + y = 8	y = 8	(0,8)
x = 1	2(1) + y = 8	2 + y = 8	y = 6	(1,6)
x = 2				
x = 3				
x = 4				

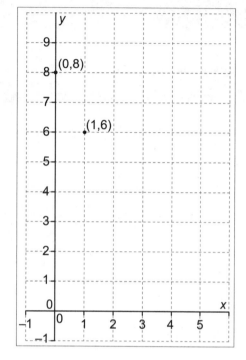

(ii) Complete the following table and, using these points, draw another line on the same graph:

	x + y = 6			Point
x = 0	(0) + y = 6	0 + y = 6	y = 6	(0,6)
x = 1				
x = 2				
x = 3				
x = 4				

(iii) Mark the point P where the two lines intersect:

$P(\_\_\_\_, \_\_\_\_)$

What do you notice? _____

2. (i) Using algebra, solve for x and y:

$x + y = 5$

$x + 2y = 8$

(ii) Complete the following table and, using these points, draw a line on the graph below:

	x + y = 5			Point
x = 0	(0) + y = 5	0 + y = 5	y = 5	(0,5)
x = 1				
x = 2				
x = 3				
x = 4				
x = 5				

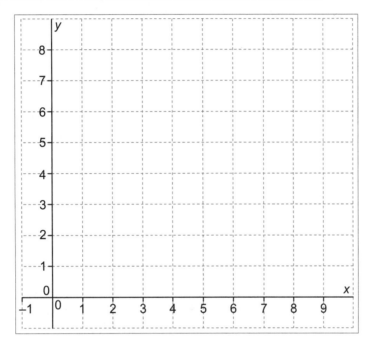

(iii) Complete the following table and, using these points, draw another line on the same graph:

	x + 2y = 8			Point
x = 0				
x = 6				

(iv) Mark the point M where the two lines intersect:

M(____, ____)

What do you notice? _____

3. Give **one** advantage and **one** disadvantage of using the graphical method to solve simultaneous equations.

Advantage:

Disadvantage:

x^2 Activity 20.1

(i) Look at the table below. In each case, write down the next **three** possible values.

The first one has been done for you:

A whole number that is:	Values
Greater than 4	5, 6, 7
Less than 2	
More than 3	
Less than or equal to 8	
Greater than 5 or equal to 5	
Less than 0	
Greater than or equal to −9	
Smaller than 11	
Bigger than or equal to −4	

(ii) Look at the table below. In each case, write down the inequality described.

The first one has been done for you:

Starting values	A whole number that is:	Or a whole number that is:
2, 3, 4, 5...	Greater than 1	Greater than or equal to 2
5, 6, 7, 8...		
18, 17, 16, 15...		
3, 2, 1, 0...		
0, −1, −2, −3...		
−1, 0, 1, 2...		
−6, −5, −4, −3, −2...		

(i) Complete the following table (the first has been done for you).

Statement	Inequality
x is greater than 4	$x > 4$
y is less than 5	
	$b \leqslant 2$
p is more than 8	
r is equal to or greater than –3	
	$m > 0$
	$n \geqslant 3$
x is less than or equal to –5	

(ii) For each numberline below, write the inequality shown.

Inequality: _____

Inequality: _____

Inequality: _____

Inequality: _____

Inequality: _____

Inequality: _____

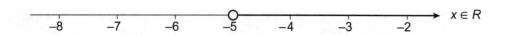

Inequality: _____

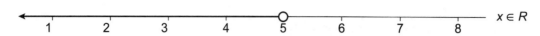

Inequality: _____

x^2 Activity 20.3

Solve each of the following inequalities by completing the tables (x is a whole number).

(i) $x + 1 > 5$

x	$x + 1 > 5$	True/False
1	Is 1 + 1 > 5?	False
2	Is 2 + 1 > 5?	False
3		
4		
5		
6		
7		

$\therefore x >$ _____

(iii) $x - 3 \geqslant 1$

x	$x - 3 \geqslant 1$	True/False
0	Is 0 − 3 ⩾ 1?	False
1		
2		
3		
4		
5		
6		

$x \geqslant$ _____

(ii) $x + 4 < 10$

x	$x + 4 < 10$	True/False
3	Is 3 + 4 < 10?	True
4		
5		
6		
7		
8		
9		

$\therefore x <$ _____

(iv) $2x + 1 \leqslant -3$

x	$2x + 1 \leqslant -3$	True/False
2	Is 2(2) + 1 ⩽ −3?	False
1		
0		
−1		
−2		
−3		
−4		

$\therefore x \leqslant$ _____

Algebraic Factors

x^2 Activity 21.1

Factorise using the HCF each of the following, using the table provided. The first one has been done for you.

(i) Factorise $3x^2 - 15x$.

Number	Factors (HCF)	Variable	Factors
3	3 × 1	x^2	$x \times x$
15	3 × 5	x	x

Answer: $3x(1x - 5)$

Check: $3x(x) - 3x(5) = 3x^2 - 15x$.

(ii) Factorise $4y^2 - 10y$.

Number	Factors (HCF)	Variable	Factors
4	2 × 2	y^2	$y \times y$
10			

Answer: _____

Check: _____

(iii) Factorise $8p + 16pq$.

Number	Factors (HCF)	Variable	Factors

Answer: _____

Check: _____

(iv) Factorise $5xy^2 - 35x$.

Number	Factors (HCF)	Variable	Factors

Answer: _____

Check: _____

(v) Factorise $4x^2y^3 + 20x^2y^2$.

Number	Factors (HCF)	Variable	Factors

Answer: _____

Check: _____

(vi) Factorise $10xy + 50xz - 60xr$.

Number	Factors (HCF)	Variable	Factors

Answer: _____

Check: _____

x^2 **Activity 21.2**

Factorise by grouping each of the following, using the table provided. The first one has been done for you.

(i) Factorise $8ax + 4ay + 12bx + 6by$.

Number	Factors (HCF)	Variable	Factors
8	4 × 2	ax	$a × x$
4	4 × 1	ay	$a × y$
12	6 × 2	bx	$b × x$
6	6 × 1	by	$b × y$

Step 1: $4a(2x + y) + 6b(2x + y)$

Step 2: $(4a + 6b)(2x + y)$

(ii) Factorise $ax + 2ay + 2bx + 4by$.

Number	Factors (HCF)	Variable	Factors

Step 1: _____

Step 2: _____

(iii) Factorise $2mp + 3mq + 2np + 3nq$.

Number	Factors (HCF)	Variable	Factors

Step 1: _____

Step 2: _____

(iv) Factorise $4axy + 2ax^2 + 2by + bx$.

Number	Factors (HCF)	Variable	Factors

Step 1: _____

Step 2: _____

(v) Factorise $ax - ab + 3bx - 3b^2$.

Number	Factors (HCF)	Variable	Factors

Step 1: _____

Step 2: _____

x^2 Activity 21.3

Factorise each of the following quadratic trinomials, using the table provided.
Part of the first one has been done for you.

(i) Factorise $x^2 + 14x + 40$.

Factors of +40	Add factors
1 × 40	1 + 40 = ___
__ × 20	__ + 20 = ___
4 × ___	4 + ___ = ___
5 × ___	5 + ___ = ___

Correct factors: $(x + \underline{})(x + \underline{})$

Now check your answer:

Now use the arrows:

$x \times x = \underline{}$ $x \times \underline{} = \underline{}x$

$\underline{} \times \underline{} = 40$ $x \times \underline{} = + \underline{}x$

$= 14x$

(ii) Factorise $x^2 + 12x + 20$.

Factors of +20	Add factors

Correct factors: $(x + \underline{})(x + \underline{})$

Now check your answer:

Now use the arrows:

$x \times x = \underline{}$ $x \times \underline{} = \underline{}x$

$\underline{} \times \underline{} = 20$ $x \times \underline{} = + \underline{}x$

$= 12x$

(iii) Factorise $x^2 + 12x + 36$.

Factors of +36	Add factors

Correct factors: $(x + \underline{})(x + \underline{})$

Now check your answer:

Now use the arrows:

$x \times x = \underline{}$ $x \times \underline{} = \underline{}x$

$\underline{} \times \underline{} = 36$ $x \times \underline{} = + \underline{}x$

$= 12x$

x^2 Activity 21.4

Factorise each of the following, using the difference of two squares:

(i) Factorise $x^2 - 25$.

$(\quad)^2 - (\quad)^2$ (two square terms)

$(\quad - \quad)(\quad + \quad)$

(ii) Factorise $y^2 - 625$.

$(\quad)^2 - (\quad)^2$ (two square terms)

$(\quad - \quad)(\quad + \quad)$

(iii) Factorise $p^2 - 900$.

$(\quad)^2 - (\quad)^2$ (two square terms)

$(\quad - \quad)(\quad + \quad)$

(iv) Factorise $r^2 - 1,000,000$

$(\quad)^2 - (\quad)^2$ (two square terms)

$(\quad - \quad)(\quad + \quad)$

Algebra: Solving Quadratic Equations

chapter **22**

x^2 Activity 22.1

1. (i) Fill in the missing factor:

- $4 \times \boxed{} = 20$
- $5 \times \boxed{} = 30$
- $2 \times \boxed{} = 14$
- $6 \times \boxed{} \times 8 = 144$

(ii) Now consider:

- $4 \times \boxed{} = 0$
- $\boxed{} \times 6 = 0$
- $100{,}000 \times \boxed{} = 0$

What do you notice about the missing factor? _____

(iii) What problem do you encounter if you are asked to fill in the following missing factors? $\boxed{} \times \boxed{} = 0$

_____

Could the two factors be the same value? _____ If yes, what value must they be? _____

x^2 Activity 22.2

Fill in the following tables to check which numbers are the correct solutions to the given equations.

(i)

Roots	Equation $x^2 - 4x = 0$			Yes/No
0	($)^2 - 4($ $) = 0$		$=$	
2	($)^2 - 4($ $) = 0$		$=$	
4	($)^2 - 4($ $) = 0$		$=$	

(ii)

Roots	Equation $x^2 + 5x = 0$			Yes/No
5	($)^2 + 5($ $) = 0$		$=$	
−5	($)^2 + 5($ $) = 0$		$=$	
0	($)^2 + 5($ $) = 0$		$=$	

(iii) You are told that one of the roots of the equation $x^2 - 7x = 0$ is 7.

What is the other root? _____

Explain how you got your answer: _____

_____

ACTIVE MATHS 1 – ACTIVITIES **161**

x^2 Activity 22.3

Fill in the following tables to check which numbers are the correct solutions of the given equations.

(i)

Roots	Equation $x^2 - 9 = 0$		Yes/No
1	$(\quad)^2 - 9 = 0$	=	
3	$(\quad)^2 - 9 = 0$	=	
–3	$(\quad)^2 - 9 = 0$	=	

(ii)

Roots	Equation $x^2 - 36 = 0$		Yes/No
6	$(\quad)^2 - 36 = 0$	=	
4	$(\quad)^2 - 36 = 0$	=	
–6	$(\quad)^2 - 36 = 0$	=	

(iii) You are told that the roots of an equation are 5 and –5.

Write down the equation: _____

Give a reason for your answer: _____

_____

x^2 Activity 22.4

Fill in the following tables to check which numbers are the correct solutions of the given equations.

(i)

Roots	Equation $x^2 - 9x + 20 = 0$		Yes/No
6	$(\quad)^2 - 9(\quad) + 20 = 0$	=	
4	$(\quad)^2 - 9(\quad) + 20 = 0$	=	
5	$(\quad)^2 - 9(\quad) + 20 = 0$	=	

(ii)

Roots	Equation $x^2 - 11x + 30 = 0$		Yes/No
5	$(\quad)^2 - 11(\quad) + 30 = 0$	=	
6	$(\quad)^2 - 11(\quad) + 30 = 0$	=	
7	$(\quad)^2 - 11(\quad) + 30 = 0$	=	

(iii)

Roots	Equation $x^2 - 2x - 3 = 0$		Yes/No
–1	$(\quad)^2 - 2(\quad) - 3 = 0$	=	
2	$(\quad)^2 - 2(\quad) - 3 = 0$	=	
3	$(\quad)^2 - 2(\quad) - 3 = 0$	=	

Algebraic Fractions

x^2 Activity 23.1

Simplify each of the following fractions by filling in the spaces provided.

(i) $\dfrac{3}{4} + \dfrac{2}{5}$

$$\frac{\boxed{}(3) + \boxed{}(2)}{\boxed{}} = \frac{\boxed{} + \boxed{}}{\boxed{}} = \frac{\boxed{}}{\boxed{}}$$

(ii) $\dfrac{1}{9} + \dfrac{3}{4}$

$$\frac{\boxed{}(1) + \boxed{}(3)}{\boxed{}} = \frac{\boxed{} + \boxed{}}{\boxed{}} = \frac{\boxed{}}{\boxed{}}$$

(iii) $\dfrac{3}{4} - \dfrac{2}{5}$

$$\frac{\boxed{}(3) - \boxed{}(2)}{\boxed{}} = \frac{\boxed{} - \boxed{}}{\boxed{}} = \frac{\boxed{}}{\boxed{}}$$

(iv) $\dfrac{4}{5} + \dfrac{1}{3} - \dfrac{3}{4}$

$$\frac{\boxed{}(4) + \boxed{}(1) - \boxed{}(3)}{\boxed{}} = \frac{\boxed{} + \boxed{} - \boxed{}}{\boxed{}} = \frac{\boxed{}}{\boxed{}}$$

x^2 Activity 23.2

Simplify each of the following fractions by filling in the spaces provided.

(i) $\dfrac{x}{3} + \dfrac{x}{4}$

LCD = _____

$$\frac{\boxed{}(x) + \boxed{}(x)}{\boxed{}} = \frac{\boxed{} + \boxed{}}{\boxed{}} = \frac{\boxed{}}{\boxed{}}$$

(ii) $\dfrac{y}{6} - \dfrac{2y}{3}$

LCD = _____

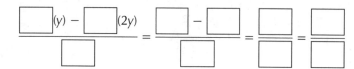

$$\frac{\boxed{}(y) - \boxed{}(2y)}{\boxed{}} = \frac{\boxed{} - \boxed{}}{\boxed{}} = \frac{\boxed{}}{\boxed{}} = \frac{\boxed{}}{\boxed{}}$$

(iii) $\dfrac{x + 1}{4} - \dfrac{2x + 1}{7}$

LCD = _____

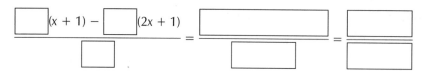

$$\frac{\boxed{}(x + 1) - \boxed{}(2x + 1)}{\boxed{}} = \frac{\boxed{}}{\boxed{}} = \frac{\boxed{}}{\boxed{}}$$

(iv) $\dfrac{2x - 1}{3} - \dfrac{3x - 1}{12}$

LCD = _____

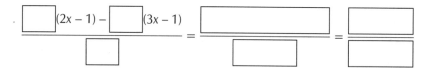

$$\frac{\boxed{}(2x - 1) - \boxed{}(3x - 1)}{\boxed{}} = \frac{\boxed{}}{\boxed{}} = \frac{\boxed{}}{\boxed{}}$$

x^2 Activity 23.3

Solve each of the following equations by filling in the spaces provided.

(i) $\dfrac{x}{2} + \dfrac{x}{4} = 3$

LCD = _____

$$\frac{\boxed{}(x)}{2} + \frac{\boxed{}(x)}{4} = \frac{\boxed{}(3)}{1}$$

$$\boxed{}(x) + \boxed{}(x) = \boxed{}(3)$$

$$\boxed{} + \boxed{} = \boxed{}$$

$$\boxed{} = \boxed{}$$

$$\boxed{} = \boxed{}$$

(ii) $\dfrac{x + 2}{4} - \dfrac{x + 1}{6} = \dfrac{3}{12}$

LCD = _____

$$\frac{\boxed{}(x + 2)}{4} - \frac{\boxed{}(x + 1)}{6} = \frac{\boxed{}(3)}{12}$$

$$\boxed{}(x + 2) - \boxed{}(x + 1) = \boxed{}(3)$$

_____

_____

_____

(iii) $\dfrac{x-2}{3} - \dfrac{x-1}{7} = 1$

LCD = _____

$$\dfrac{\boxed{}(x-2)}{3} - \dfrac{\boxed{}(x-1)}{7} = \dfrac{\boxed{}(1)}{1}$$

$$\boxed{}(x-2) - \boxed{}(x-1) = \boxed{}(1)$$

_____

_____

_____

_____

x^2 Activity 23.4

Simplify each of the following algebraic fractions by filling in the spaces provided.

(i) $\dfrac{4x^3}{2x}$

$= \dfrac{4 \times x \times x \times x}{2 \times x} = $ _____

(ii) $\dfrac{10x^2y}{2y}$

$= \dfrac{10 \times \boxed{} \times \boxed{} \times \boxed{}}{2 \times \boxed{}} = $ _____

(iii) $\dfrac{18x^2y^2}{9y^3}$

$= \dfrac{\boxed{} \times \boxed{} \times \boxed{} \times \boxed{} \times \boxed{}}{9 \times \boxed{} \times \boxed{} \times \boxed{}} = $ _____

(iv) $\dfrac{90y^4}{10xy^3}$

$= \dfrac{\boxed{} \times \boxed{} \times \boxed{} \times \boxed{} \times \boxed{}}{\boxed{} \times \boxed{} \times \boxed{} \times \boxed{} \times \boxed{}} = $ _____

(v) $\dfrac{50a^3b^2c}{25abc^2}$

$= \dfrac{\boxed{} \times \boxed{} \times \boxed{} \times \boxed{} \times \boxed{} \times \boxed{} \times \boxed{}}{\boxed{} \times \boxed{} \times \boxed{} \times \boxed{} \times \boxed{}} = $ _____

Geometry III: Further Theorems

 Activity 24.1

Using a protractor, identify the pairs of similar triangles. Label each angle measurement in the diagram below.

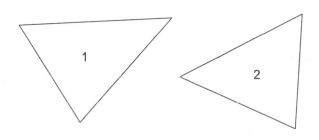

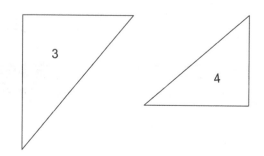

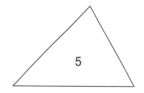

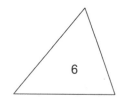

(i) Triangle _____ is similar to triangle _____.

(ii) Triangle _____ is similar to triangle _____.

(iii) Triangle _____ is similar to triangle _____.

(iv) Explain what we mean by saying that two triangles are similar.

_____

_____

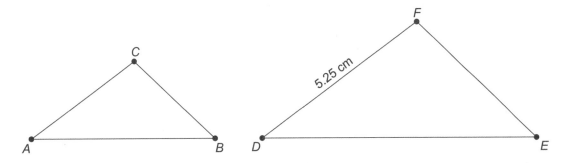

(i) Using a protractor, measure all the angles in both triangles.

Triangle *ABC*	Corresponding angle in triangle *DEF*
$|\angle A|$ =	$|\angle D|$ =
$|\angle B|$ =	$|\angle E|$ =
$|\angle C|$ =	$|\angle F|$ =

(ii) What do you notice about the corresponding angles in the pair of similar triangles?

_____

(iii) Using a ruler, measure:

Triangle *ABC*	Corresponding side in triangle *DEF*
$|AB|$ =	$|DE|$ =
$|BC|$ =	$|EF|$ =
$|AC|$ =	$|DF|$ = 5.25 cm

(iv) Now work out the following, writing your answers as fractions in simplest form:

$\dfrac{|AB|}{|DE|}$ =	$\dfrac{|DE|}{|AB|}$ =
$\dfrac{|BC|}{|EF|}$ =	$\dfrac{|EF|}{|BC|}$ =
$\dfrac{|AC|}{|DF|}$ =	$\dfrac{|DF|}{|AC|}$ =

(v) What do you notice about the relationship between the corresponding sides in the pair of similar triangles?

_____

(vi) In the box provided, write down a rule (theorem) that sums up what you have learned so far in this activity.

Theorem

Using a protractor and ruler, identify the pairs of congruent triangles. **Show your measurements for each triangle on the figures below**.

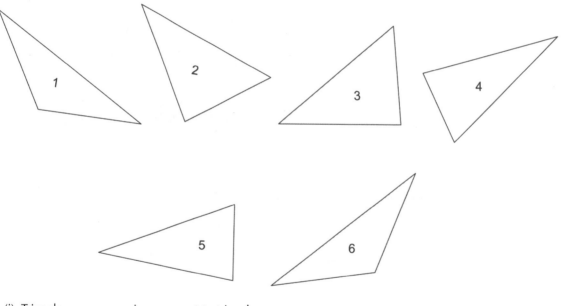

(i) Triangle _____ is congruent to triangle _____.

(ii) Triangle _____ is congruent to triangle _____.

(iii) Triangle _____ is congruent to triangle _____.

(iv) Explain what we mean by saying that two triangles are congruent.

_____

_____

GEOMETRY III: FURTHER THEOREMS

Using a protractor and ruler, show that the following triangles are congruent.
Explain how you showed that the triangles are congruent.

(i)

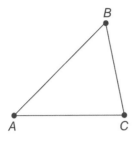 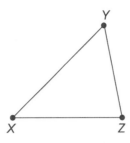

|AB| =	|BC| =	|AC| =
|XY| =	|YZ| =	|XZ| =

Reason for congruence: _____

(ii)

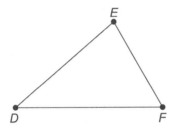 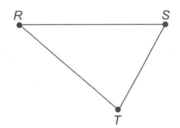

|∠EDF| =	|∠EFD| =	|DF| =
|∠TRS| =	|∠RST| =	|RS| =

Reason for congruence: _____

(iii)

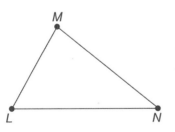 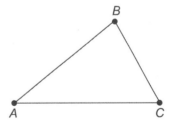

|LM| =	|LN| =	|∠MLN| =
|BC| =	|AC| =	|∠ACB| =

Reason for congruence: _____

(iv)

$|XY| =$	$|YZ| =$	$|\angle XZY| =$
$|RQ| =$	$|PR| =$	$|\angle QPR| =$

Reason for congruence: _____

Activity 24.5

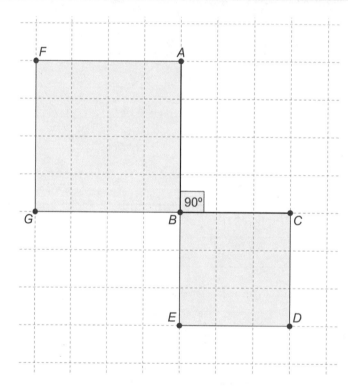

(i) What shape is *ABGF*? _____

What is its area (in square centimetres)? _____

(ii) What shape is *DCBE*? _____

What is its area (in square centimetres)? _____

(iii) Draw a line segment from *A* to *C*.

What type of triangle is *ABC*? _____

(iv) Measure $|AC|$. _____

 (v) Write down the area of a square with side length $|AC|$. _____

(vi) Add the areas from parts (i) and (ii). _____

     Is the answer equal to your answer in part (v)? _____

     What name could you give to the side [AC]?

     _____

 Activity 24.6

Construct a triangle ABC with the following sides: $|AB| = 8$ cm, $|BC| = 6$ cm and $|AC| = 10$ cm.

(i) Find:

$|AB|^2 =$
$|BC|^2 =$
$|AB|^2 + |BC|^2 =$

(ii) Now find:

$|AC|^2 =$

     What do you notice? _____

(iii) How does this show that the triangle *ABC* is a right-angled triangle?

_____

(iv) Check your answer by using a protractor.

(v) Which side is opposite the right angle? _____

Activity 24.7

1. (i) Mark a point *C* on the circle below. Now draw triangle *ABC*.

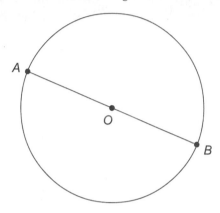

(ii) If *O* is the centre of the circle, what is the name for the line segment [*AB*]? _____

(iii) Measure the angle *ACB*: |∠*ACB*| =

2. (i) Mark a point *E* on the circle below and then draw triangle *DEF*.

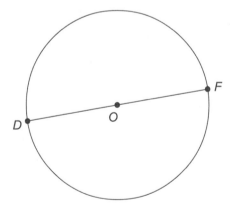

(ii) Measure the angle *DEF*: |∠*DEF*| =

(iii) In the box provided, write down a corollary that states what you have learned so far in this activity.

Corollary:

(i)

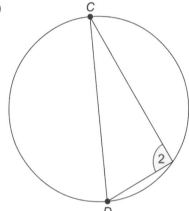

$|\angle 1| = $ _____

$\therefore [AB]$ is the _____ of the circle.

(ii)

$|\angle 2| = $ _____

$\therefore [CD]$ is the _____ of the circle.

(iii)

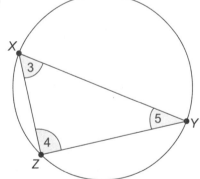

$|\angle 3| = $ _____

$\therefore [ZY]$ is the diameter of the circle.   True/False

$|\angle 4| = $ _____

$\therefore [XY]$ is the diameter of the circle.   True/False

$|\angle 5| = $ _____

$\therefore [XZ]$ is the diameter of the circle.   True/False

(iv) In the box provided, write down a corollary that states what you have learned so far in this activity.

Corollary:

Activity 25.1

Construct a triangle *DEF* where $|DE| = 5$ cm, $|DF| = 10$ cm and $|EF| = 7$ cm.

Sketch	Construction

■ Check your construction using a ruler.

■ Measure all three angles to the nearest degree:

$|\angle EDF| = $ _____

$|\angle FED| = $ _____

$|\angle DFE| = $ _____

What do they add up to?

_____

 ## Activity 25.2

Construct a triangle *ABC* having $|AB| = 8$ cm, $|\angle BAC| = 55°$ and $|AC| = 6$ cm.

Sketch	Construction

■ Check your construction using a ruler and protractor.

■ Measure the other two angles in the triangle to the nearest degree, and measure the line segment [BC] to the nearest millimetre.

$|\angle ABC| = $ _____

$|\angle ACB| = $ _____

$|BC| = $ _____

Construct a triangle *PQR* where |*PR*| = 9 cm, |∠*QPR*| = 45° and |∠*QRP*| = 50°.

Sketch	Construction

- Check your construction using a ruler and protractor.
- Measure the third angle in the triangle to the nearest degree, and measure the line segments [*PQ*] and [*QR*] to the nearest millimetre.

|∠*PQR*| = _____ |*PQ*| = _____ |*QR*| = _____

 Activity 25.4

Construct a triangle *ABC* where |*AB*| = 5 cm, |*AC*| = 7 cm and |∠*ABC*| = 90°.

Sketch	Construction

- Check your construction using a ruler and protractor.
- Measure the remaining two angles in the triangle to the nearest degree, and measure the line segment [*BC*] in centimetres to one decimal place.

|∠*BAC*| = _____ |∠*ACB*| = _____ |*BC*| = _____

 **Activity 25.5**

Construct a triangle *PQR* where $|RQ| = 7.5$ cm, $|\angle RPQ| = 50°$ and $|\angle PQR| = 90°$.

Sketch	Construction

- Check your construction using a ruler and protractor.
- Measure the line segments [*PQ*] and [*PR*] in millimetres.

  $|PQ| = $ _____ $|PR| = $ _____

 Activity 25.6

Construct a triangle *XYZ* where $|XY| = 9$ cm, $|\angle XZY| = 90°$ and $|\angle XYZ| = 25°$.

Sketch	Construction

- Check your construction using a ruler and protractor.
- Measure the line segments [*XZ*] and [*YZ*] to the nearest millimetre.

  $|XZ| = $ _____ $|YZ| = $ _____

Using a **protractor** and **ruler**, construct the rectangle WXYZ where |WX| = 7 cm and |XY| = 3 cm.

Sketch	Construction

 Activity 25.8

Construct a rectangle ABCD, where |AB| = 9 cm and |BC| = 4 cm.

Sketch	Construction

CONSTRUCTIONS II

Activity 26.1

1. In the diagram below, each point is labelled with a letter.

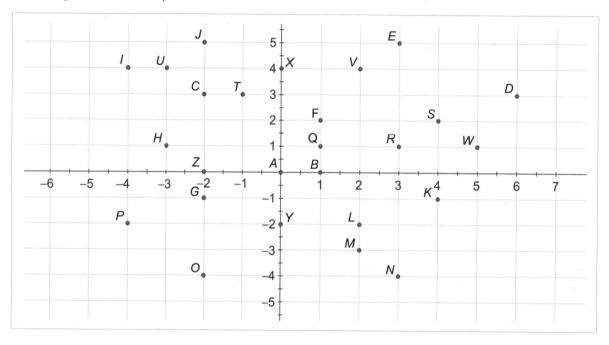

(i) Replace the points with the correct letters from the graph to reveal famous landmarks and famous locations.

(ii) Match each landmark with its correct location by drawing an arrow.

Landmark
(−1,3)(−3,1)(3,5)   (−1,3)(0,0)(−2,5) (2,−3)(0,0)(−3,1)(0,0)(2,−2)
(3,5)(2,−3)(−4,−2)(−4,4)(3,1)(3,5) (4,2)(−1,3)(0,0)(−1,3)(3,5) (1,0)(−3,4)(−4,4)(2,−2)(6,3)(−4,4)(3,−4)(−2,−1)
(3,5)(−4,4)(1,2)(1,2)(3,5)(2,−2) (−1,3)(−2,−4)(5,1)(3,5)(3,1)
(−2,3)(−2,−4)(2,−2)(−2,−4)(4,2)(4,2)(3,5)(−3,4)(2,−3)
(−4,−2)(0,−2)(3,1)(0,0)(2,−3)(−4,4)(6,3)(4,2)

Location
(3,1)(−2,−4)(2,−3)(3,5)
(3,5)(−2,−1)(0,−2)(−4,−2)(−1,3)
(3,−4)(3,5)(5,1) (0,−2)(−2,−4)(3,1)(4,−1)
(−4,4)(3,−4)(6,3)(−4,4)(0,0)
(−4,−2)(0,0)(3,1)(−4,4)(4,2)

2. (i) Now it's your turn! Using the same graph, write down the co-ordinates that will spell out the names of four cities (excluding the three cities from Q. 1).

	Location
(1)	
(2)	
(3)	
(4)	

(ii) Now ask the person beside you to solve your puzzle.

	City
(1)	
(2)	
(3)	
(4)	

Activity 26.2

1. Study the right-angled triangle *ABC* shown below.

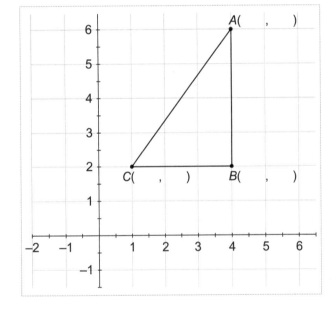

(i) Fill in the co-ordinates *A*, *B* and *C*.

(ii) What is the length of [*AB*]? _____.
Show this length on the diagram.

(iii) What is the length of [*CB*]? _____.
Show this length on the diagram.

(iv) It is now possible to find the length of [*AC*] using the theorem of P _____.

(v) Find the length of [*AC*]:

$$|AC|^2 = |BC|^2 + |AB|^2$$
$$|AC| = \sqrt{(\quad)^2 + (\quad)^2}$$
$$|AC| = \sqrt{(\quad) + (\quad)}$$
$$|AC| = \sqrt{\quad}$$
$$|AC| =$$

2. Consider the right-angled triangle *PQR*.

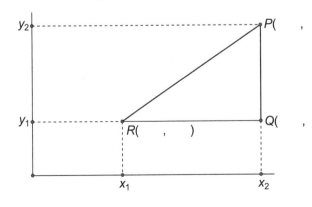

(i) Fill in the co-ordinates of *P*, *Q* and *R* on the diagram.

(ii) What is the length of [*PQ*]? _____

(iii) What is the length of [*RQ*]? _____

(iv) Find the length of [*PR*].

$$|PR|^2 = |RQ|^2 + |PQ|^2$$
$$\therefore |PR| = \sqrt{(\quad)^2 + (\quad)^2}$$

We use this formula to find the distance between two points.

Activity 26.3

1. Using your compass, bisect the line segments to find the midpoints. Show the co-ordinates of the midpoint of each line segment on the diagram.

> You will need a compass for this activity.

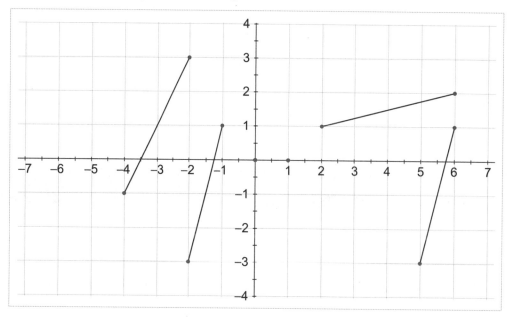

2. In statistics we get the mean of two numbers by adding the numbers together and dividing our answer by 2. On a numberline, the mean of two numbers is the midpoint of the two numbers.

(i) For each of the following numberlines, indicate the midpoint of the two highlighted points:

(a)

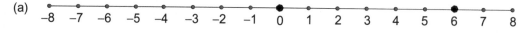

(b)

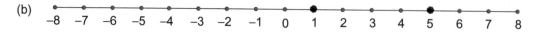

(c)

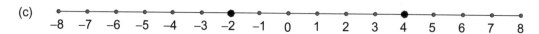

(d)

(e)

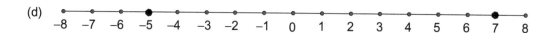

(f)

(ii) Confirm your answers to part (i) by finding the mean of the two highlighted numbers on each numberline:

(a) Mean =	(d) Mean =
(b) Mean =	(e) Mean =
(c) Mean =	(f) Mean =

3. Consider the line segment [AB], shown below.

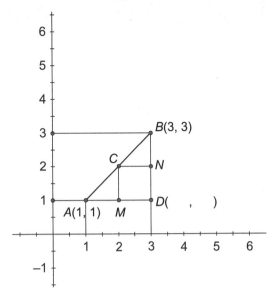

(i) On the graph, fill in the co-ordinates of the point D.

(ii) What are the co-ordinates of M, the midpoint of [AD]? M(,).

(iii) What are the co-ordinates of N, the midpoint of [BD]? N(,).

(iv) Hence, write down the co-ordinates of C.
C = (,).

4. Consider the line segment [AB], shown below.

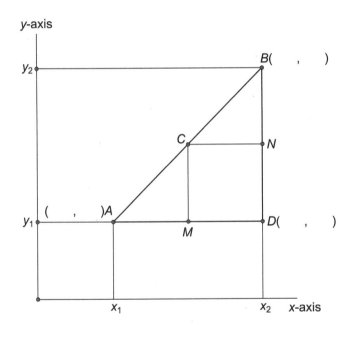

(i) On the graph, fill in the co-ordinates of the points A, B and D.

(ii) What are the co-ordinates of M, the midpoint of [AD]?

(iii) What are the co-ordinates of N, the midpoint of [BD]?

(iv) Hence, write down the co-ordinates of C.

C is the midpoint of [AB]. You will find this formula on page 18 of *Formulae and Tables*.

1. Consider the line shown below.

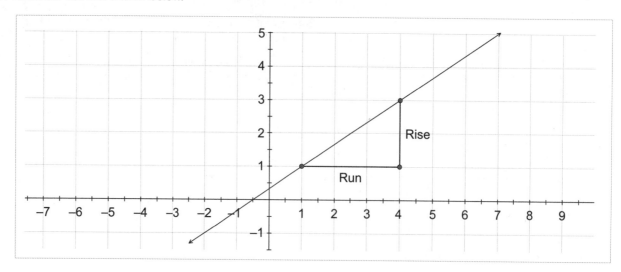

(i) From the graph, find the rise and the run of the line.

Rise =	Run =

(ii) What is the slope of the line?

Slope = $\dfrac{\text{Rise}}{\text{Run}}$ =

2. Using the grid below, draw lines with the following slopes:

(i) $\dfrac{1}{2}$　　(ii) $\dfrac{3}{2}$　　(iii) $-\dfrac{1}{4}$　　(iv) $-\dfrac{6}{5}$

3. Lines that have positive slope rise from left to right. Lines that have negative slope fall from left to right. Lines that are horizontal have zero slope. Study the graph below, and then say which lines have positive slope, which have negative slope and which have zero slope.

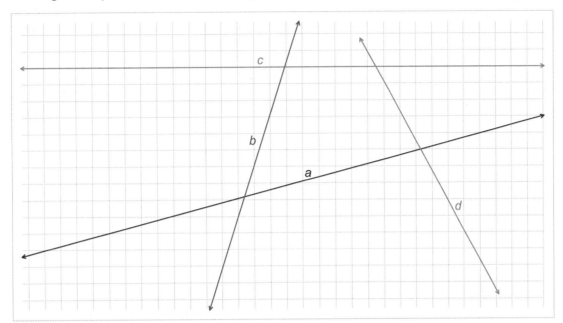

Positive slope	Negative slope	Zero slope

4. Consider the line *AB*, shown below.

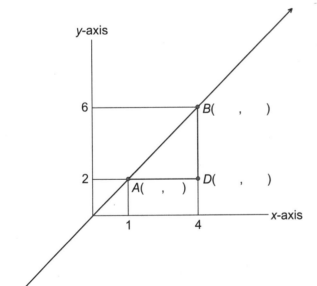

(i) On the graph, fill in the co-ordinates of the points *A*, *B* and *D*.

(ii) What is the length of the line segment [*AD*]?

_____

(iii) What is the length of the line segment [*BD*]?

_____

(iv) Hence, write down the slope of the line *AB*.

5. Consider the line *AB*, shown below.

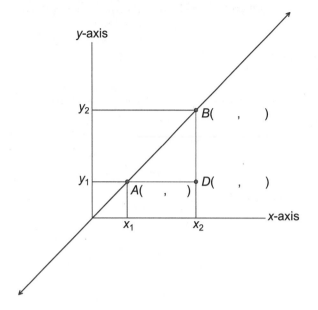

(i) On the graph, fill in the co-ordinates of the points *A*, *B* and *D*.

(ii) What is the length of the line segment [*AD*]?

_____

(iii) What is the length of the line segment [*BD*]?

_____

(iv) Hence, write down the slope of the line *AB*.

This formula finds the slope of a line. You will find it on page 18 of *Formulae and Tables*.

6. The diagram below shows two pairs of parallel lines.

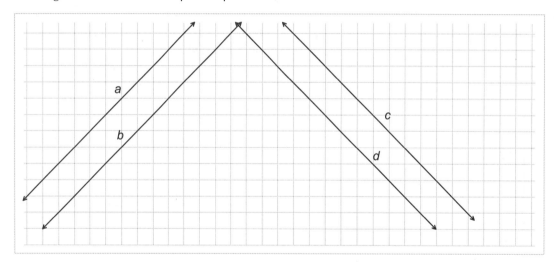

(i) Find the slope of each of the lines.

Slope of *a*	Slope of *b*	Slope of *c*	Slope of *d*

(ii) What can you say about the slope of lines that are parallel?

1. Find two points on each of the following lines. Then graph the lines carefully using graph paper.

(i) $y = 2x$

(iii) $y = -2x$

(ii) $y = 3x$

(iv) $y = 4x$

2. Find the slope of each line in Q. 1. Use either the slope formula on page 18 of *Formulae and Tables*, or use your graph.

(i)

(ii)

(iii)

(iv)

3. Considering your answers to Q. 1 and Q. 2, what is the connection between the slope of the line and its equation?

_____

_____

4. In Question 3, you should have discovered that lines of the form $y = mx$ have slope m. We will now consider lines of the form $y = mx + c$. By letting $x = 0$, find where the following lines cross the y-axis:

(i) $y = 3x + 4$

(iii) $y = \frac{3}{4}x - 2$

(ii) $y = -2x - 3$

(iv) $y = \frac{2}{3}x + 5$

You should now see that the constant term, or number, at the end of the equation gives the y-intercept (the point where the line crosses the y-axis).

5. Graph the following lines. Begin by plotting the point where the line crosses the y-axis. Then find another point on the graph, using the rise and run of the slope.

(i) $y = \frac{3}{4}x - 2$ (ii) $y = \frac{5}{6}x + 1$ (iii) $y = -2x + 3$ (iv) $y = 2x$

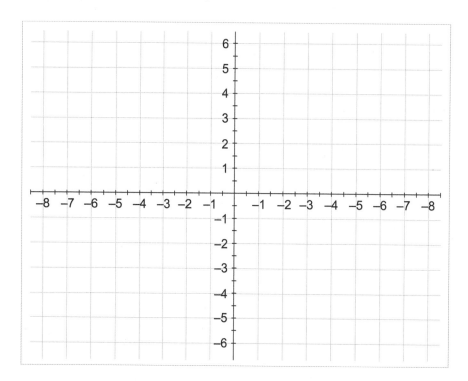

Activity 27.1

Consider the following shape:

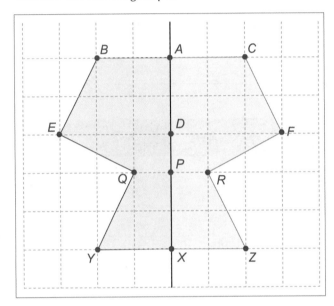

(i) Name the line of symmetry. _axis_

(ii) Measure the following distances:

|AB| = 2 cm	|AC| = 2 cm
|DE| = 3cm	|DF| = 3cm
|PQ| = 1cm	|PR| = 1 cm
|XY| = 2cm	|XZ| = 2 cm

What do you notice? _same distance_
either side of point on axis

(iii) Draw an axis of symmetry for each of the following shapes:

Number of axes of symmetry: 1	Number of axes of symmetry:

(iv) Describe in your own words what a line of symmetry is.

a line that can divide
a shape in half

(v) Draw a line of symmetry for the following letter:

(vi) Consider the letter now. Draw a line of symmetry for the letter.

Did the number of lines of symmetry change?

_No_

Complete the following shapes using the line of symmetry given.

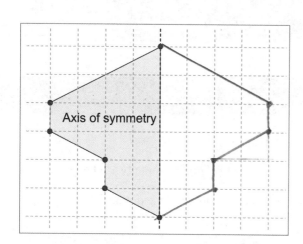

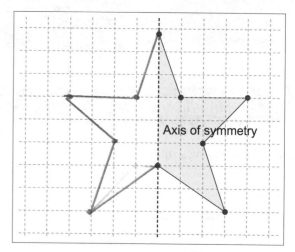

The triangle *DEF* has been moved by the translation which maps *X* onto *Y*.

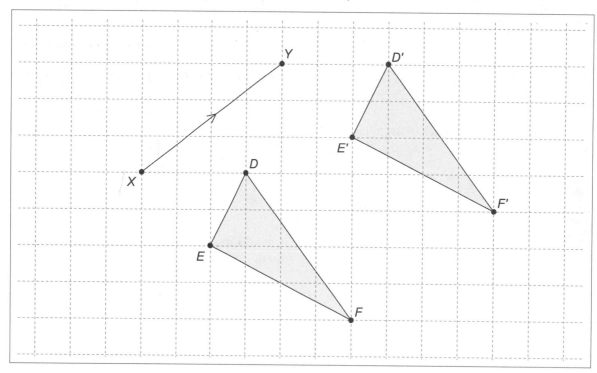

(i) Explain what the notation *D'* means. _Image of O_

TRANSFORMATION GEOMETRY

(ii) Measure the following distances:

Object	Image
|DE| = 2cm	|D'E'| = 2cm
|DF| = 5cm	|D'F'| = 5cm
|FE| = 4.5 cm	|F'E'| = 4.5 cm

What do you notice? _Same_

(iii) Measure the following distances:

|XY| =	5cm
|DD'| =	5cm
|EE'| =	5cm
|FF'| =	5cm

What do you notice? _Same_

(iv) Name one property of a translation. _Identical & faces same way_

(v) Complete the following table. The first row has been done for you.

Translation	Distance moved right/left	Distance moved up/down
$X \rightarrow Y$	4 right	3 up
$D \rightarrow D'$	4 right	3 up
$E \rightarrow E'$	4 right	3 up
$F \rightarrow F'$	4 right	3 up

What do you notice? _Same_

(vi) The same triangle DEF is now moved under the translation which maps Y onto X $(\overrightarrow{YX})$.

On the diagram below, draw the image of this triangle under this translation.

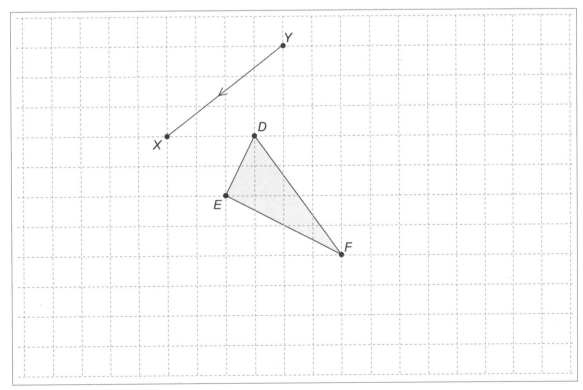

The triangle *ABC* has been moved under a central symmetry in the point *P*.

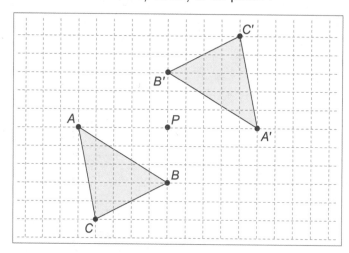

(i) Measure the following distances:

Object	Image
|AB| = 3 cm	|A'B'| = 3 cm
|AC| = 2.5 cm	|A'C'| = 2.5 cm
|BC| = 2 cm	|B'C'| = 2 cm

Does the length of the triangle sides change under a central symmetry? __No__

(ii) What do you notice about the image? __It is the same just upside down.__

(iii) Measure the following distances:

Object	Image
|AP| = 2.5 cm	|A'P| = 2.5 cm
|BP| = 1.5 cm	|B'P| = 1.5 cm
|CP| = 3 cm	|C'P| = 3 cm

What do you notice? _____

Activity 27.5

The parallelogram *ABCD* has a centre of symmetry *E*.

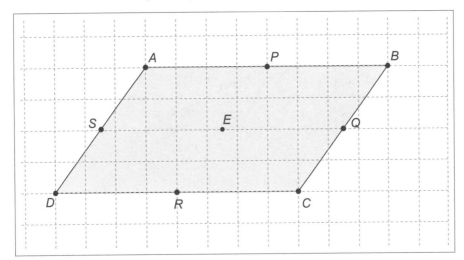

(i) Measure the following distances:

|AE| = 2.5cm	|EC| = 2.5 cm
|PE| = 2cm	|ER| = 2cm
|BE| = 5cm	|ED| = 5cm
|QE| = 3.5cm	|ES| = 3.5cm

What do you notice? ___Same_____

(ii) What other name could be given to the point *E*? __centre of symmetry__

(iii) On the diagram below, find the centre of symmetry of the shape. Label this as the point *C*.

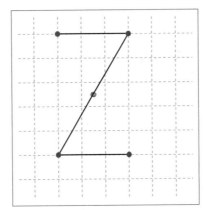

(iv) Explain how you would check your answer.

___check if the length between each point and centre point matches the length of the point opposite.___

The triangle *DEF* has been moved under an axial symmetry in the x-axis.

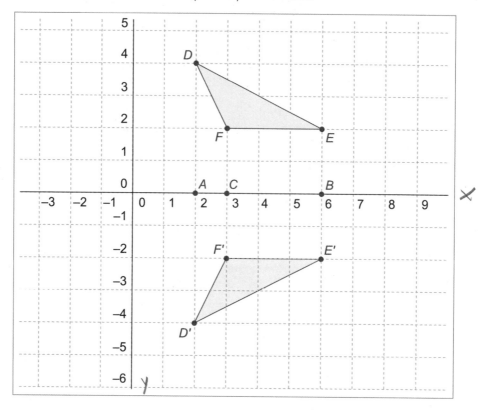

(i) On the diagram, label the x-axis and the y-axis.

(ii) Measure the following distances:

Object	Image
|FE| = 2·5cm	|F'E'| = 2·5cm
|DF| = 2cm	|D'F'| = 2cm
|ED| = 4cm	|E'D'| = 4cm

Does the length of the triangle sides change under an axial symmetry? ___No___

(iii) Measure the following:

First distance	Second distance
|DA| = 3·5cm	|AD'| = 3·5cm
|EB| = 1·5cm	|BE'| = 1·5cm
|FC| = 1·5cm	|CF'| = 1·5cm

What do you notice? ___Same___

(iv) Complete the following table. The first row has been done for you:

		Change in x sign	Change in y sign
D = (2,4)	D' = (2,−4)	No	Yes
E = (6 , 2)	E' = (6 , −2)	No	Yes
F = (3 , 2)	F' = (3 , −2)	No	Yes

What do you notice? __Only change in y-axis__

(v) On the diagram below, move the triangle *PQR* under an axial symmetry in the y-axis.

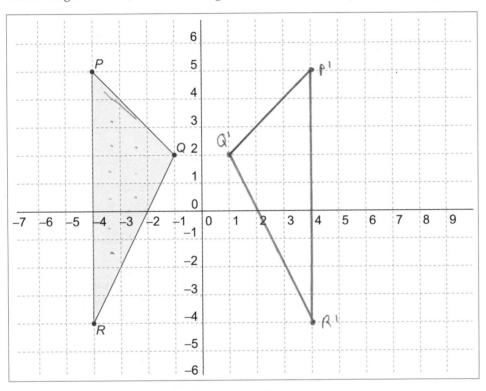

(vi) Write down the co-ordinates of the following:

		Change in x sign	Change in y sign
P = (−4, 5)	P' = (4 , 5)	Yes	No
Q = (−1, 2)	Q' = (1 , 2)	Yes	No
R = (−4, −4)	R' = (4 , −4)	Yes	No

What do you notice? __Only change in x__

(vii) Calculate the area of Δ*PQR*. _____

Calculate the area of Δ*P'Q'R'*. _____

What do you notice about the area of the triangles?

_____ Same _____

Activity 28.1

1. For each of the following triangles, name the right angle and the hypotenuse.

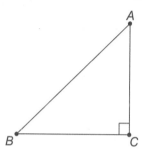

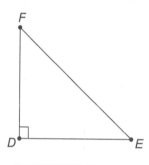

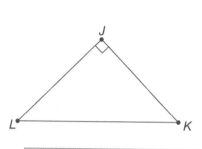

Right angle =

Hypotenuse =

Right angle =

Hypotenuse =

Right angle =

Hypotenuse =

2. Pythagoras said that *the area of the square on the hypotenuse is equal to the sum of the areas of the squares on the other two sides.* Use the theorem of Pythagoras to find the value of X in the diagrams below:

(i)

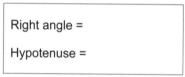

(ii)

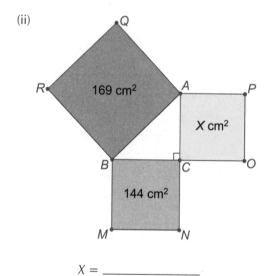

$X =$ _____

$X =$ _____

3. Complete the following table. The first row gives the length of a side in a square. You need to find the area of the square and put your answers in the second row.

Length of side (cm)	1	5	9	11	15	20	25
Area of square (cm²)							

4. Complete the following table. The first row gives the area of a square.
You need to find the length of a side in the square and put your answers in the second row.

Area of square (cm²)	4	49	64	100	121	169	10,000
Length of side (cm)							

5. For each of the diagrams in Q. 2, find $|AC|$, $|BC|$ and $|AB|$.

(i)

$|AC| =$ $\qquad$ $|BC| =$ $\qquad$ $|AB| =$

(ii)

$|AC| =$ $\qquad$ $|BC| =$ $\qquad$ $|AB| =$

Activity 28.2

1. In each of the following right-angled triangles, write down the length of the side **opposite** angle A, the length of the side **adjacent** to angle A, and the length of the **hypotenuse**.

(i)

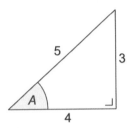

Opposite =

Adjacent =

Hypotenuse =

(ii)

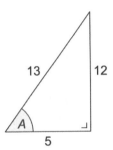

Opposite =

Adjacent =

Hypotenuse =

(iii)

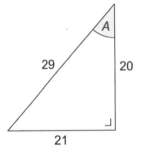

Opposite =

Adjacent =

Hypotenuse =

(iv)

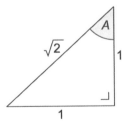

Opposite =

Adjacent =

Hypotenuse =

(v)

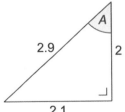

Opposite =

Adjacent =

Hypotenuse =

(vi)

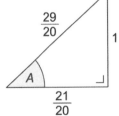

Opposite =

Adjacent =

Hypotenuse =

2. Here are three right-angled triangles. Each has an angle of 30°.

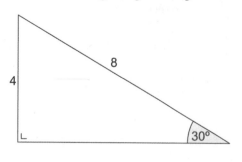 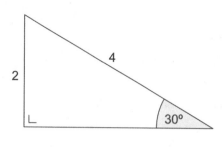 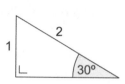

(i) Write down the fraction $\dfrac{\text{opposite}}{\text{hypotenuse}}$ for each triangle. Give your answer in simplest form.

(ii) What do you notice? _____

_____

3. A right-angled triangle contains an angle of measure 30°. If the length of the opposite side is 10 cm, what is the length of the hypotenuse?

As you can see, the fraction $\dfrac{\text{opposite}}{\text{hypotenuse}}$ is always $\dfrac{1}{2}$ for a right-angled triangle containing an angle of size 30°. We call this fraction sin 30°. **So sin 30° = $\dfrac{1}{2}$.**

4. In Q. 3, we saw that sin 30° = $\dfrac{1}{2}$. We can find the sin of any angle as follows:

- Construct a right-angled triangle containing the angle.
- Measure the length of the opposite and the hypotenuse.
- Calculate the fraction $\dfrac{\textbf{opposite}}{\textbf{hypotenuse}}$.

(i) Construct a right-angled triangle containing the angle 20°.

(ii) Now calculate sin 20° by measuring the length of the opposite side and the length of the hypotenuse.

sin 20° =

5. Now use your calculator to find sin 20° correct to one decimal place.

sin 20° =

6. Right-angled triangles have two other ratios called cos and tan. For an angle A in a right-angled triangle,

we say that $\cos A = \dfrac{\text{adjacent}}{\text{hypotenuse}}$ and $\tan A = \dfrac{\text{opposite}}{\text{adjacent}}$.

Using the triangle you constructed in Q. 4, find cos 20° and tan 20°.

tan 20° =	cos 20° =

7. Now use your calculator to find cos 20° and tan 20° correct to one decimal place.

cos 20° =	tan 20° =

To summarise: $\sin A = \dfrac{\text{opposite}}{\text{hypotenuse}}$ $\cos A = \dfrac{\text{adjacent}}{\text{hypotenuse}}$ $\tan A = \dfrac{\text{opposite}}{\text{adjacent}}$

Activity 28.3

For this activity you will need a clinometer and measuring tape.
Pick six elevated points around your school and find the height above floor level of each point.

Point	Angle of elevation	Length of adjacent

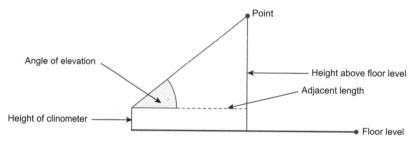

In your calculations, ensure you deal with the height of the clinometer.

Point	Height above floor level

Solving Problems Using Algebra

x^2 Activity 29.1

(i) If x is a number, write an expression for each of the following:

Number plus two	$x + 2$
Number minus 10	
Five added to the number	
Two subtracted from the number	
Two times the number	
Three times the number, then add one	
Four times the number, then add four	
The number squared	
The number squared, then six subtracted	
Five times the number squared	

(ii) Write the following expressions as mathematical sentences:

$4x$	Four times a number
$2x + 1$	
$3y - 7$	
$2 + x$	
$9 - 3x$	
$x^2 - 3$	
$y^2 + 4$	
$x^2 - 4x$	
$a^2 - a + 4$	
$2y + y^2$	

(i) Write an equation for each of the following and solve for the unknown.

Statement	Workings	Answer
Five times a number plus one is equal to 11.		Number =
10 times a number plus 15 add up to 35.		Number =
Four times a number minus 2 is equal to 26.		Number =
€5 is paid towards the cost of three CDs. There is still €16 to be paid.		Cost of one CD =
I put €20 in a ticket machine. I received three tickets and €8 in change.		Cost of one ticket =

(ii) Write the following equations as mathematical sentences and solve for the unknown. For each one, make up a different unknown.

Equation	Sentence	Workings
$4x = 16$	Four shirts cost €16.	
$5x + 7 = 27$		
$3x - 5 = 13$		
$2x = 5 + x$		
$4x + 5 = 2x + 11$		

(i) The sum of two numbers is 10. Their difference is 4. By filling in the table and solving the simultaneous equations, find the two numbers.

Let x = the bigger number and let y = the smaller number.

Word equation	Maths equation
The sum of two numbers is 10.	
Their difference is 4.	

Solve these two simultaneous equations:

x = the bigger number. $\therefore x =$ _____.　　　　y = the smaller number. $\therefore y =$ _____.

(ii) A phone company charges x cents for a text and y cents for a picture message.

Four text messages and three picture messages cost €1.82. Ten text messages and one picture message cost €1.30. By filling in the table and solving the simultaneous equations, find the cost of each type of message:

Let $x =$ _____, and let $y =$ _____.

Word equation	Maths equation

Solve these two simultaneous equations:

$x =$ _____　　　　　　$y =$ _____

x^2 **Activity 29.4**

(i) A number is squared and five times the number is added to this, then three is subtracted to give a total of 11.

Find two possible values for the number.

Let x be equal to a number.

Fill in the following table.

A number is squared	Five times the number is added	Three is then subtracted	=	11

Solve to find the unknown numbers.

Now check your answer.

Answers	A number is squared	Five times the number is added	Three is then subtracted	=	11	True/False

(ii) The side lengths of a rectangle are shown.

$x + 7$

$x + 3$

(a) By filling in the following table, write an expression for the area of this rectangle.

$(x + 7)(x + 3)$

	x	$+7$
x	x^2	
$+3$		$+21$

Expression: _____

(b) If the area of the rectangle is equal to 77 m^2, find the length of each side.

Workings

SOLVING PROBLEMS USING ALGEBRA

chapter 30

Functions

Activity 30.1

(a) (i) Complete the input–output table.

Input	Rule: Add 5 to the input	Output
2	2 + 5	
3		
4		

(ii) List the couples for the completed table.

Couples: $\left\{ \left(2, \boxed{}\right), \left(3, \boxed{}\right), \left(4, \boxed{}\right) \right\}$

(iii) Draw a mapping diagram for the given relation.

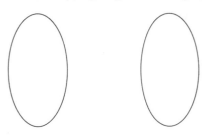

(b) (i) Complete the input–output table.

Input	Rule: Twice the input and subtract 2	Output
1	$2\left(\boxed{}\right) - 2$	
2		
−4		

(ii) List the couples for the completed table.

Couples: $\left\{ \left(1, \boxed{}\right), \left(2, \boxed{}\right), \left(-4, \boxed{}\right) \right\}$

(iii) Draw a mapping diagram for the given relation.

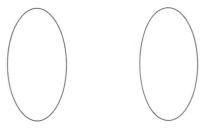

(c) (i) Complete the input–output table.

Input	Rule: Square the input and add 2	Output
1		
−3		
4		

(ii) List the couples for the completed table.

Couples: $\left\{ \left(\boxed{}, \boxed{}\right), \left(\boxed{}, \boxed{}\right), \left(\boxed{}, \boxed{}\right) \right\}$

(iii) Draw a mapping diagram for the given relation.

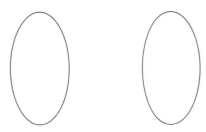

Activity 30.2

For each question:

(i) Write the rule using function notation.

(ii) Complete the input–output table.

(iii) Write down the answers to the remaining questions.

(a) Rule: 'Add 4 to the input.' $f(x) =$ [   ]

x	f(x) =	y
1		
2		
3		

∴ $f(1) =$ [ ] , $f(2) =$ [ ] , $f(3) =$ [ ]

(b) Rule: 'Double the input and then subtract 3.' $f(x) =$ [   ]

x	f(x) =	y
0		
2		
−2		

∴ $f(0) =$ [ ] , $f(2) =$ [ ] , $f(-2) =$ [ ]

Range = { [ ] , [ ] , [ ] }

(c) Rule: 'Square the input then add 3.' $g(x) =$ [   ]

x	g(x) =	y
−3		
2		
5		

∴ $g(-3) =$ [ ] , $g(2) =$ [ ] , $g(5) =$ [ ]

Domain = { }

Range = { }

Graphing Functions

 Activity 31.1

1. (i) Complete the following input–output table:

x	f(x) = 2x + 1	y	Couple
–3	2(–3) + 1	–5	(–3,–5)
–2			
–1			
0			
1			
2			
3			

(ii) Now plot these couples on the co-ordinate plane. (The first one has been done for you.)

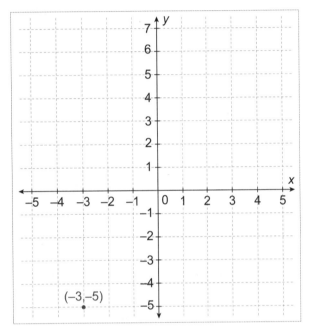

(iii) Use your ruler to connect all the points (or couples).

(iv) At what point does the graph of f(x) = 2x + 1 cross the y-axis?

2. (i) Complete the following input–output table:

x	f(x) = –x + 4	y	Couple
–3	–(–3) + 4	7	(–3,7)
–2			
–1			
0			
1			
2			
3			

(ii) Now graph this line on the diagram above (in Question 1, part (ii)).

(iii) At what point does the graph of $f(x) = -x + 4$ cross the y-axis?

(iv) The y-intercept is where the graph of the function crosses the y-axis.
What is common about the y-intercept for both functions shown?

_____

_____

(v) At what point do the graphs of the two functions meet?

 Activity 31.2

(i) Complete the following input–output table:

x	$f(x) = x^2 + 2x - 3$	y	Couple
−4	$(-4)^2 + 2(-4) - 3$	5	(−4,5)
−3			
−2			
−1			
0			
1			
2			

(ii) Now plot these points on the diagram shown.

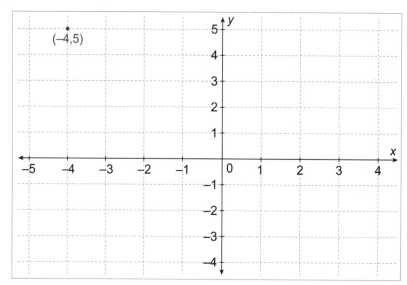

(iii) Join the points with a smooth curve, using the order in which they appear in your table.

(iv) At what point does the graph of $f(x) = x^2 + 2x - 3$ cross the y-axis?

Activity 31.3

The graph of the function $f(x) = x^2 - 5x + 4$ is shown.

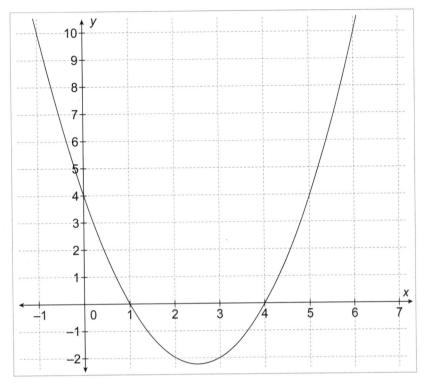

(i) Mark on the graph the two points where the function intersects the x-axis.
Label these points A and B.

Point $A = ($, $)$ Point $B = ($, $)$

∴ The values of x for which $f(x) = 0$ are:

$x = $ _____   and $x = $ _____

(ii) Draw the line $y = 4$. Mark on the graph the two points where this line intersects the graph of the **function** f.
Label these points C and D.

Point $C = ($, $)$ Point $D = ($, $)$

∴ The values of x for which $f(x) = 4$ are:

$x = $ _____   and $x = $ _____

(iii) Draw the line $x = 6$. Mark on the graph the point where this line intersects the graph of the **function** f.
Label this point E.

Point $E = ($, $)$

∴ The value of $f(6)$ is: $y = $ _____

What other value of x will give the same answer as $f(6)$? _____

Activity 31.4

(i) Complete the following input–output table:

x	f(x) = x²	y	Couple
−3	(−3)²	9	(−3,9)
−2			
−1			
0			
1			
2			
3			

(ii) Now plot these points on the diagram shown and graph $f(x) = x^2$.

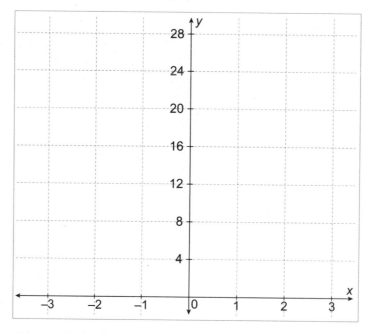

(iii) Now complete the following tables:

x	f(x) = 2x²	y	Couple
−3	2(−3)²	18	(−3,18)
−2			
−1			
0			
1			
2			
3			

x	f(x) = 3x²	y	Couple
−3	3(−3)²	27	(−3,27)
−2			
−1			
0			
1			
2			
3			

(iv) Now sketch the graphs of $y = 2x^2$ and $y = 3x^2$ on the same diagram as $y = x^2$.

(v) In general, as the coefficient of the x^2 term gets bigger, the graph gets _____.

What point is common to all three functions? [ ]

(vi) Explain why this point is common to all three functions. _____

_____

Activity 31.5

The graph of the function $f(x) = x^2$ is shown.

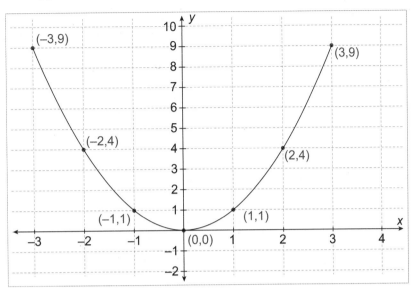

(i) Complete the following tables:

x	$f(x) = x^2 + 1$	y	Couple
–3	$(-3)^2 + 1$	10	(–3,10)
–2			
–1			
0			
1			
2			
3			

x	$f(x) = x^2 - 2$	y	Couple
–3	$(-3)^2 - 2$	7	(–3,7)
–2			
–1			
0			
1			
2			
3			

(ii) Now draw the graphs of $f(x) = x^2 + 1$ and $f(x) = x^2 - 2$ on the same diagram as $f(x) = x^2$.

(iii) ▪ Every point on the graph of the function $f(x) = x^2 + 1$, when compared to the graph of $f(x) = x^2$, has been

moved _____ by _____ unit.

▪ Every point on the graph of the function $f(x) = x^2 - 2$, when compared to the graph of $f(x) = x^2$, has been

moved _____ by _____ units.

(iv) ▪ At what point does the graph of the function $f(x) = x^2 + 1$ cross the y-axis?

▪ At what point does the graph of the function $f(x) = x^2 - 2$ cross the y-axis?

▪ What is the link between the function and where it crosses the y-axis?

_____

▪ In general, a change in the value of the constant b of a function of the form $f(x) = x^2 + b$ will shift the graph

of $f(x) = x^2$ _____ or _____ .

Activity 31.6

The graph of the function $f(x) = x^2$ is shown.

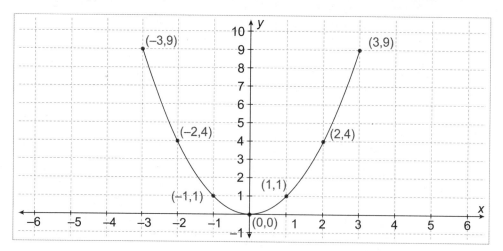

(i) Complete the following tables:

x	$f(x) = (x-3)^2$	y	Couple
0	$(0-3)^2$	9	(0,9)
1			
2			
3			
4			
5			
6			

x	$f(x) = (x+2)^2$	y	Couple
−5	$(-5+2)^2$	9	(−5,9)
−4			
−3			
−2			
−1			
0			
1			

(ii) Draw the graphs of $f(x) = (x-3)^2$ and $f(x) = (x+2)^2$ on the same diagram as $f(x) = x^2$.

(iii) ▧ Every point on the graph of the function $f(x) = (x-3)^2$, when compared to the graph of $f(x) = x^2$, has been moved _____ by _____ units.

▧ Every point on the graph of the function $f(x) = (x+2)^2$, when compared to the graph of $f(x) = x^2$, has been moved _____ by _____ units.

(iv) ▧ At what point does the graph of the function $f(x) = (x-3)^2$ touch the x-axis? [ ]

▧ At what point does the graph of the function $f(x) = (x+2)^2$ touch the x-axis? [ ]

▧ What do you notice? _____

(v) ▧ At what point does the graph of the function $f(x) = (x-3)^2$ cross the y-axis? _____

▧ At what point does the graph of the function $f(x) = (x+2)^2$ cross the y-axis? _____

▧ What do you notice? _____

▧ In general, a change in the value of the constant b of a function of the form $y = (x+b)^2$ will shift the graph _____ or _____.

Solving Problems Graphically

chapter **32**

1. (i) Using the following points, draw each line on the graph paper:

Line *p*	A (–4,0)	B (0,2)
Line *q*	C (0,6)	D (12,0)

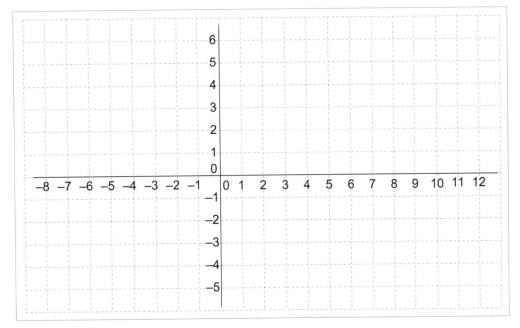

Mark on your graph the point of intersection of the two lines:

Point of intersection = (_____ , _____)

(ii) On the same graph, plot the points (0,0) and (8,2), and use these points to draw the line *r*.

Mark on your graph the points of intersection of this new line with the lines *p* and *q*:

Points of intersection = (_____ , _____) and (_____ , _____)

(iii) Complete the following table to show where the lines intersect each other:

	Line *p*	Line *q*	Line *r*
Line *p*	////////////		
Line *q*		/////////////	
Line *r*			/////////////

2. By completing the following table, plot each line on the graph paper provided and identify where they intersect.

$3x + 2y = 12$	
Let $x = 0$.	Let $y = 0$.
If $x = 0$, then $y =$ _____.	If $y = 0$, then $x =$ _____.
Point (0,___)	Point (___,0)

$y = \frac{1}{2}x + 2$	
Let $x = 0$.	Let $y = 0$.
If $x = 0$, then $y =$ _____.	If $y = 0$, then $x =$ _____.
Point (0,___)	Point (___,0)

Point of intersection = (,   )

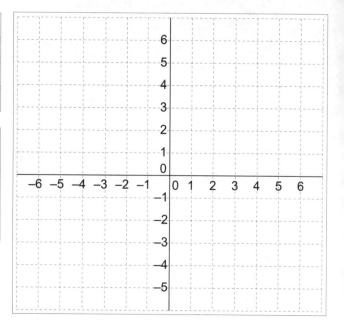

 Activity 32.2

The equation that represents the fare for a taxi journey is $y = x + 3$.

- ▪ x represents the distance travelled in kilometres.

- ▪ y is the cost of the fare in euro.

Complete the given table and then draw a graph using the x-values and y-values from the table.

Distance travelled (x-value)	$y = x + 3$	Cost (y-value)
0		
2		
4		
6		
8		
10		

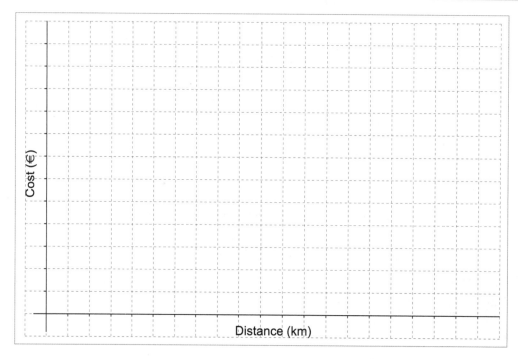

(i) Use your graph to find the cost of a 7 km taxi journey. _____

(ii) How far could you travel for €9? _____

(iii) What is the cost of just hiring the taxi? _____

On the graph, this corresponds to the _____.

(iv) How much does the cost of the fare change per kilometre? _____

This corresponds to the _____.

(v) Using the following table, find the cost of each journey:

Distance travelled (*x*-value)	*y* = *x* + 3	Cost (*y*-value)
10		
15		

Activity 32.3

Mary is thinking of switching phone companies. She has the choice of two:

- Talk and Walk charges 4 cents per minute plus a 20 cents per call connection fee.

- Fast Talk charges 8 cents per minute with no connection fee.

  (i) Complete the given table to show how much each company charges.

	Talk and Walk	Fast Talk
Connection fee		
1 min		
2 mins		
3 mins		
4 mins		
5 mins		
6 mins		

  (ii) Graph the information given in this table. Let the *x*-axis on your graph represent time (minutes) and the *y*-axis cost (cents).

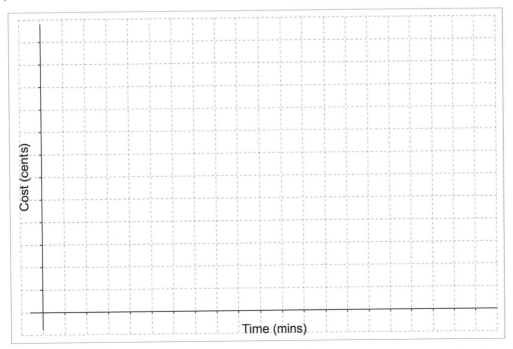

(iii) How is a connection fee represented on the graph?

_____

(iv) How long is a call that costs the same using either company? _____

How is this represented on the graph? _____

(v) If Mary takes on average 3 minutes per call, which company should she use?

_____

(vi) Which phone company's graph is directly proportional? _____

 ## Activity 32.4

A pond's area is measured, as it is liable to flood. The area in square metres covered by the pond over a five-day period is recorded. The pond begins to flood after Day 0.

Day	Area (m²)
0	10
1	16
2	20
3	22
4	22
5	20

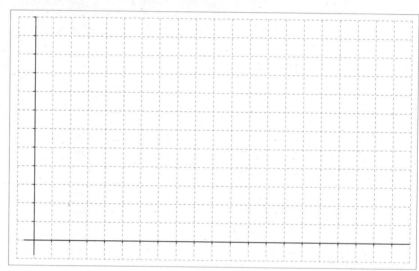

(i) Draw a graph to represent this table.

(Let the x-axis represent time and the y-axis represent area.)

Is the graph a straight line or a curve? _____

(ii) Complete the following table:

Day	Change in area
0–1	
1–2	
2–3	
3–4	
4–5	

(iii) What type of pattern does this represent?

_____

_____

Give a reason for your answer.

_____

_____

(iv) After how many days did the flood waters start to recede?

_____